PELICAN BOOKS

KT-419-535

J. L. Houlden was born in 1929, educated at Altrincham Grammar School and read modern history and theology at the Queen's College, Oxford. Ordained in 1955, he served for three years as curate at St Mary's, Hunslet, Leeds, and was then on the staff of Chichester Theological College from 1958 to 1960. From 1960 to 1970 he was Chaplain Fellow of Trinity College, Oxford, since when he has been Principal of Cuddesdon Theological College. He is the author of *Paul's Letters from Prison* (Pelican New Testament Commentaries) and has contributed to a number of essay collections.

Ethics and the New Testament

*

J. L. HOULDEN

PENGUIN BOOKS

Penguin Books Ltd, Harmondsworth, Middlesex, England
Penguin Books Inc., 7110 Ambassador Road, Baltimore, Maryland 21207, U.S.A.
Penguin Books Australia Ltd, Ringwood, Victoria, Australia

—

First published 1973

—

Copyright © J. L. Houlden, 1973

—

Made and printed in Great Britain by
Cox & Wyman Ltd, London, Reading and Fakenham
Set in Linotype Pilgrim

For Jim and Sally
David and Sarah
John and Patricia

Contents

Acknowledgements

The author is grateful to the theological students at Oxford for whose needs he had to work for the conclusions presented in this book; to Dennis Nineham, the Warden of Keble College, for helpful suggestions and encouragement; to Peter Strange for correcting the proofs; and to Patricia Richardson for compiling the indexes.

Cuddesdon, 1971   J. L. H.

Introduction

ENLIGHTENED Christians believe that the benighted regard the New Testament as a source of ethical instruction and little else. Yet even the enlightened, who know that the ethics depend on the theology, are capable of using the New Testament as an oracle on ethical questions in ways that we can only suppose they have not had the leisure fully to consider. There seems to be room for a patient examination of the assumptions on which not only the use but also the exposition of the ethical teaching of the New Testament ought to rest.

The New Testament must first be understood in its own context – on that most would agree. So: within what climate of thought did its writers live? What forces affected their consideration of ethical questions? What standpoints did they themselves adopt? What evidence do they give of the solutions worked out by the first christian congregations to the moral problems confronting them? Finally, what use are their ideas and solutions to us, living in quite different times, yet sharing their christian allegiance or looking to them for guidance? These are the questions with which this book is concerned.

It begins therefore with an attempt to establish, partly in the contrasting light of other approaches, a way of looking at the moral teaching of the New Testament which does not do violence to the insights and methods of modern New Testament study. Writers on this subject have not always succeeded in this matter. Their failure has something to do with the fact that this aspect of the New Testament is often studied in connection with moral theology rather than New

Testament studies. Moral theology has its own agenda and methods, and it is easy for the New Testament material of interest to it to be forced to dance, methodologically speaking, to its tune.

We go on to examine the place of ethics in the context of the religious forces at work in the world of the New Testament. Concern with morals in isolation was rare. It was constantly being mixed with other interests and impulses, and it flourished, to a large extent, on their terms.

The next part of the book seeks to identify the standpoint on ethical matters of most of the major New Testament writers. We resist the idea that there is such a thing as 'the New Testament view'. For clarity's sake, we must distinguish one writer from another and let the voice of each be heard. We try to show what part ethics played in these writers' schemes of things.

Then we select a number of practical moral problems which faced Christians of the early period and analyse the range of solutions which they reached. Behind the writers and the Church that faced the questions lies Jesus; how far may we know what he really taught and what he stood for? And finally, we ask: what good is all this to us? Is it in any way authoritative, and even if we decide that it is, how can we use it in practice?

This book aims to meet two needs. Students are often required to turn to the study of ethics, including biblical ethics, after they have made themselves familiar with the critical study of the Bible. They do not always find it easy to get their bearings as they come to look at the Bible from this fresh point of view. More general readers may want to know not just what the New Testament has to say about ethical matters but how they might regard this material and how they might use it once they have discovered how to handle it.

Finally, we do not aim to give an exhaustive account of New Testament ethics: not all ethical texts appear in the index of references. This book is about the *shape* of New Testament ethics. It hopes to be an aid towards comprehension.

1. The Shape

DISPIRITING as it is, we must start by questioning the work on which we now embark. It is far from clear that the ethical teaching of the New Testament is a valid or useful subject for independent study. This is one example of a more general hesitation. Whenever there is a proposal to discuss 'the x of the New Testament', it is proper to raise two cautionary points.

First, it is important to inquire whether the topic in question can be isolated from the whole theological outlook of the New Testament without distorting both. The answer will not always be the same. It is possible to examine the flora or the topography of Palestine, as evidenced in the Gospels, without any such risk: the subject can stand on its own feet. In a case like the demonology of the New Testament, it may just be possible, at least as far as some aspects of the matter are concerned, but it borders on the dangerous; for what the New Testament writers think about the demonic is integrally connected with what they think about God and about the universe. When it comes to the Christology of the New Testament or the New Testament's teaching about creation or the Church, then a man writes at considerable peril. It is not possible to deal with these matters satisfactorily apart from the rest of New Testament thought. Undoubtedly the ethics of the New Testament fall into this category. So, in persisting we urge that the wider picture is not for a moment forgotten, and we ourselves shall attempt not to lose sight of it. Our subject cannot profitably be viewed in isolation from its theological context.

Second, there is, strictly, no such thing as 'the x of the New Testament', or, at least, if it can be produced, it is a murky and uncertain blend. 'The x of the New Testament' can, after all, only be made out of 'the x' of each several writer, even of each book. It is only at the cost of ignoring the individuality of each, in thought and expression, that the unified account can emerge. But then the distinct flavours, worth savouring in isolation and having a right to their independence, are absorbed into the mixture, and lost. If this is nevertheless to be done, it can only be for one of two reasons: either because the individuality has not been acknowledged or appreciated, or because of some overwhelmingly compelling dogma about the authoritativeness of the New Testament canon as such. More defensibly, from the point of view of historical scholarship, investigation may convince a man that individuality does not mean diversity, at least not on such a scale that it is misleading to produce something that can be labelled 'the teaching of the New Testament on x'. The present writer is doubtful whether, in most cases, such an account can usefully be constructed. In any case, the point to establish is that the individual writer is the starting-point. There can be no initial assumption of harmony. Each thinks and writes in his own way, on the basis of his own concerns, in the setting of his own formation and his own christian community. 'The x of the New Testament', in other words, is either an abstraction or a perversion, with the most doubtful basis in New Testament scholarship.

In venturing to write on the moral teaching of the New Testament, then, we need to see it always in the closest relation to the New Testament's message as a whole; and, as far as method is concerned, we are to investigate the teaching of each of the main writers in turn, not assuming that they necessarily sing in unison or even in harmony. From the point of view of the strict historical study of the New Testament, the idea of the canon, as a collection of writings accorded religious authority, is an anachronism. The New Testament writers were not, like the contributors to a volume of essays, men consciously engaged on a cooperative venture. They wrote for their own reasons in their own circumstances, unaware of the future role of their work. In so far as any of them were aware of any of the rest, their purpose seems to have been to correct and supersede them rather than to complement them (cf. p. 47).

In the light of these cautionary remarks, how may we proceed in the study of the moral teaching of the New Testament? It will help to make our own method clear if, for the sake of comparison, we describe the methods used by others.

In the past it has not been uncommon for writers on the ethics of the New Testament to approach their subject from the side of moral theology as a whole, having in mind that discipline's accustomed programme of topics: conscience, natural law, the motive of reward, the quest for perfection, casuistry, and the traditional virtues and vices. With their agenda fixed, they have then turned to the New Testament for material. It is as if they said: 'We know what moral theology is. Let us see what the New Testament has to say about it.'[1] This procedure cannot avoid the charge of being needlessly and misleadingly indirect – if what interests us is the inner movement of the thought of the New Testament writers in their historical setting. If that is our concern, then

1. The early chapters of K. E. Kirk, *The Vision of God* (London, 1931) show some signs of this approach, alongside others that come closer to taking the writings on their own terms. So, to a degree, does C. Spicq, *La Théologie Morale du Nouveau Testament* (Paris, 1965), though his themes are more closely dictated by the New Testament itself than by the traditional scope of moral theology.

we can work closer to them than this, and have no need to approach them through such an artificial construction as the syllabus of moral theology which has been built up over the centuries.

Even when there is a more direct approach, however, there is still room for variation. R. Schnackenburg, for example, in *The Moral Teaching of the New Testament* (Herder; Burns & Oates, 1965), undoubtedly operates 'at ground level': he sets out to show what Jesus and the early Church taught. His book has three parts: (i) the moral teaching of Jesus; (ii) the moral teaching of the early Church in general; (iii) the teaching of prominent individuals, e.g. Paul, John and James.

His scheme is open to serious objection. When we come to the New Testament and endeavour to come to terms with it, we are confronted with a set of writings, and these alone are our primary evidence. That for which they are primary evidence is, strictly, the thought of the writer concerned, or at most the circle which he represents. Here then is our proper starting-point – that which for Schnackenburg is the finishing-point. Behind particular writers, we can discern, with varying degrees of confidence, something of the attitudes of groups in the early Church. In the gospels in particular we believe that we have material which, before it reached its final version in the work of the evangelists, had been used and inevitably moulded by the churches over some decades, in accordance with their convictions and their needs. Only through these two influencing and modifying agents can we approach the mind and teaching of the historical Jesus himself. To him all the writers bear witness, but it is only secondarily that they provide evidence for our knowledge of him; and generally, the more precise we wish to be about him, the more tentative we have to be. Jesus, in other words, is to be found at the end not at the beginning of an inquiry such as Schnackenburg has conducted. His order needs to be reversed, if the New Testament is to convey what it has to teach.

There is perhaps no need to labour the point, but it may be helpful to suggest how confusion in the matter of method arises so easily. It results, so it seems, from a failure to distinguish between the theological and the evidential witness of the New Testament. Clearly, the writings witness theologically to Jesus himself as the one sent by God; but as documents from the past they witness, as we have said, first to the writer's thought, then to the early Church which stands behind him, and only then to Jesus. Nothing good can come from confusing the two modes of witness, and if we wish to understand the New Testament on its own terms, there is no doubt that we must begin with the historical witness. Equally there is no doubt that the theological witness proves on investigation to involve a wide range of questions and to be related to the historical witness by ties of great complexity. This is an area not to be entered lightly, and only when historical preparations are complete.

Before we embark on the study of the New Testament writers themselves, let us ask what position ethics occupied in their world of thought. How important was it to them to think explicitly about moral problems, or would this very notion be foreign to them? Were ethical questions central or peripheral? How far was their place affected first by general features of the intellectual or religious climate, and second by factors in the christian faith itself?

The study of ethics, at its widest, concerns man's moral attitudes and aspirations, and the processes by which he makes decisions on questions of conduct. It involves the analysis of ideas about what is good and what is evil, and the analysis of situations where duty is not clear.

Viewed as an independent domain, ethical study and

analysis are of maximum power when either of two conditions is present. First, atheism, provided that it avoids non-religious metaphysical systems such as Marxism, renders ethics wholly autonomous. If they are to survive at all as the object of serious thought, then they must do so unaided. They can look for illumination in data about society or human psychology, but these will only eliminate errors springing from crassness or ignorance. They will enable judgements to be informed, but they will not help in themselves to produce decisions or arguments about values. This must be done in total independence. There can be no falling back upon outside metaphysical aids, such as the commands of God, no appeal to metaphysical goals, such as the vision of God, which would make certain lines of conduct desirable. There may indeed be moral ideals and moral rules, but they will stand independently of divine sanctions and be built upon a structure of purely moral argument.

Second, when men believe in a universe wholly ordered on the basis of regular laws – without special divine interventions, without an imminent end, and without close providential supervision – then too ethics come into their own as a largely autonomous realm. In such a universe, men give maximum value to the principles of order and stability, and take the highest view of the independent worthwhileness of human affairs. There may indeed be God-given rules, but their importance lies more in their status as rules, fixed and stable, than in their derivation from God.

Under either of these conditions, ethics are autonomous, or virtually so, and possess their greatest significance in the motivation of human living. In these circumstances, men will characteristically turn to moral arguments when they consider the issues confronting them, and even such deep matters as the purpose and goal of their lives. They will be likely to have two overriding aspirations: excellence in all aspects of their conduct; and, from the more subjective point of view, the fulfilment of themselves in a virtuous, harmonious existence. The qualities that will be admired and promoted are those which make for stability in the satisfying of these aspirations. Goodness will be whatever leads to the smooth working of happy personal and social life; vice will be whatever spoils or impedes it. Aristotle's city-state, as described in the *Politics*, is a classical example of these aims and their practical expression.

In the New Testament the first of our two conditions (atheism) never appears as an assumption, but the second (belief in a regular cosmos) does so occasionally. In the world of the time, Stoicism was one of a number of philosophical systems which exhibited this kind of thinking, and there are some signs of Stoic influence in the area of practical morals, especially classifications and listings of virtues and vices. However, it cannot be claimed that the conditions for the autonomy of ethics are ever satisfactorily fulfilled in the New Testament.

Indeed a number of major religious forces which operated powerfully in the New Testament world of thought threatened the autonomy of ethics; that is to say, they made it unlikely that men who accepted christian allegiance would see life as a self-contained quest for virtue. They would be likely to prefer to express their dominant objective in other terms, and see moral aims as within the context of them and dependent upon them. These forces did not affect all New Testament writers in equal degree. They do not even affect the same writer consistently through the whole range of his work, and sometimes a writer is influenced by forces which are scarcely consistent. Some have minimal effect or exert influence largely by provoking reaction. But all are present in the New Testament atmosphere, and unless we take account of them we shall not grasp the lines along which the moral thinking of the first Christians ran.

1. *The devaluing of the material world.* In the period which concerns us (and in the centuries which immediately followed), pessimism about the world, about life within it, and above all about physical existence, dominated the religious consciousness of more and more sections of Mediterranean society. Diverse philosophical and religious systems, spreading from the Orient, shared the same obsessive despair about the physical universe.[2] Judaism, with its strong tradition of belief in a Creator whose work was good, had resources with which to offset the prevailing tendency. *Au fond*, it succeeded in doing so; and so, by inheritance and common conviction, did the christian Church. Nevertheless, neither was immune, and we shall find within the New Testament literature evidence of its influence. When this literature was written, the most systematic developments of this pessimistic religious feeling still lay just in the future: the gnostic systems of the second and third centuries. But all the ingredients were already present.

In this atmosphere, where the world was regarded as evil or valueless, and man's only hope lay in escaping from it or rendering himself, as far as possible, impervious to its influence, moral striving for objectives and ideals within the world lost all point. Ethical argument ceased to have that stable background of significant experience which is a condition of its seriousness. To proclaim human ideals was to utter meaningless cries in a mocking or unheeding universe.

2. See E. R. Dodds, *Pagan and Christian in an Age of Anxiety* (Cambridge, 1965), and H. Jonas, *The Gnostic Religion* (Boston, 1958). Educated classical pagans held to a robust optimism more effectively than most (cf. Peter Brown, *The World of Late Antiquity* (London, 1971) pp. 49ff.).

Salvation could only come from without. No process of self-improvement within this world, with its relationships and its intricacies of behaviour, could possibly contribute to this outcome, for the divine, the only source of salvation, had not one whit of concern for the fabric and setting of human life.

Many of those who felt this with particular keenness, like the members of the gnostic sects, devoted themselves to the strictest asceticism. But it would be quite false to see this as a treading of the path of virtue, an element in a moral ascent which had meaning and was to bear fruit within this life. It was rather a gesture of contempt in the face of the world and of hatred for its demonic creator. Not surprisingly, then, others indulged with equal fervour, on the basis of the same beliefs, in extreme libertinism, in a spirit of insolent, defiant bravado. Equally with the asceticism, it was a gesture against a valueless and meaningless world. Either policy served. Where life in the world has lost all value, virtue and vice cease to have meaning. Ethics are no longer current coin. The words of I John ii, 15f., taken in isolation, are not far from this point of view: 'Love not the world, neither the things that are in the world ... For all that is in the world, the lust of the flesh, and the lust of the eyes, and the pride of life, is not of the Father, but is of the world.' As we shall see, the Johannine standpoint is by no means fully represented in this quotation, but it is nevertheless one strand.

2. *Expectation of the imminent end of the world.* Conceptually speaking, this expectation, entertained with the utmost dramatic urgency by many Jews, especially those of Palestine, at this period, was not wholly unrelated to this depreciation of the material world. In so far as it involved a flight from an oppressive present reality and a search for a salvation which issued from other realms, it may not unfairly be seen as the jewish expression of the

prevailing pessimism. But there were differences. Those affected by the gnostic tendency were making a judgement about the total universe, here and now, as they experienced it, and in the face of it were making an act of metaphysical abhorrence. Jews moved by apocalyptic speculation looked rather towards the future for their way out, to the coming catastrophic intervention of God. This act would transform all things, through unspeakable suffering and relentless judgement; but it would nevertheless be an intervention in this world and in this world's history, and so 'apocalyptic' never quite lost an element of this-worldly hope. The historical and, however qualified, this-worldly quality in apocalyptic derived from the jewish theological tradition, with its affirmation of God's role as creator of all things. This tradition persisted *formally* unimpaired by the elements of dualistic thinking which had become so prominent in Judaism in the last centuries of the pre-christian era.

One effect of this conjunction of elements was that concern with questions of conduct did not diminish. Quite the reverse. Even those Jews who were most deeply affected by the fever of apocalyptic devoted themselves to the study and observance of the Law with unprecedented rigour, partly because they believed that such obedience would itself hasten the coming of the day of God's intervention for which they longed. Indeed, the very prospect of judgement is always likely to be a stimulus to morals (Rom. ii, 15f.).

It is, however, not surprising that this expectation should have repercussions in some areas of moral thinking. Behaviour is bound to be affected if you believe that the order of the world is about to be dissolved. Long-term aspirations and duties lose their force, and special measures are called for. New Testament writers, for whom the triumphant appearance of Christ, ushering in the End, is imminent, show many signs of such repercussions.

For example, in II Thessalonians iii, 7–10, Paul is replying to Christians who – unless it is simply that they are idle – feel that the nearness of Christ's return removes the normal need and obligation to work. Paul, with commonsense logic ('If any one will not work, let him not eat'), denies the inference. On another question, however, that of marriage, Paul, subjected to the same doctrinal pressures, reacts quite differently. In I Corinthians vii, he gives it as his considered view, after careful and balanced argument, that in the present emergency, Christians are ill-advised to enter upon matrimony (verse 26), and those who are married would do well to abstain from sexual relations (verses 29ff.). In the former case, he decides that the interruption of customary duties is unwarranted; in the latter case, he positively enjoins it. Judgement could go either way.

There is a comparable contrast between two aspects of Paul's attitude to relations with the state. In I Corinthians vi, 1ff., he chides Christians who take their disputes with each other to the civil law-courts; not only because it is bad to expose quarrels within the brotherhood to the public gaze, but also because when the End comes – as come it soon will – they, the Christians, will join with their Lord in the judging of the whole world, including the angels. In them will be fulfilled the role accorded to the saints of the Most High in Daniel (vii, 22, 26f.). Are they then to find the settling of their own petty disputes beyond their competence?

Yet in Romans xiii, 1ff., a different attitude appears. No longer does the coming End to earthly political authority mean that its claims and powers may already be ignored. No longer is the Church to withdraw itself from the due processes of government. Rather, Christians are to pay their taxes as good citizens, and the imperial power is said to have the sanctions of God at its back (verse 2).

These contradictory attitudes appear to betoken

considerable uncertainty in arriving at a standpoint from which to judge practical moral questions. Such uncertainty need cause us no surprise. It is natural that when it came to giving practical counsel, now the imminence of the End, now the demands of the day-to-day life should be uppermost. The former emphasis deals a crippling blow to the ordinary processes of ethical argument, the latter makes them still necessary.

In the first generations, Christians often attached much of the significance of the coming End, as God's decisive intervention, to the life and particularly to the death and resurrection of Jesus. Concepts and language reflected this conviction. It left its mark, even with regard to ethical attitudes, on the telling of the story of the Passion of Jesus. Thus in both the Gospel of Mark (xiv, 4–7) and in that of John (xii, 4–8), the normal duty of generosity to the poor is suspended in view of Jesus' impending death. The anointing of Jesus by the woman is commended, partly as a sign which foreshadows his burial, and partly as a beautiful act done to him in this solemn hour, where God is crucially at work for man's salvation.

In the Gospel of Luke, for whom the Passion of Jesus has, by contrast, lost some of this atmosphere of crisis and for whom the return of Christ is further away, so it seems, than it had been for Paul and probably for Mark, this incident is transferred from the Passion narrative to a point in the course of Jesus' ministry (vii, 36ff.); and from being an act which signifies the temporary abrogation of a moral duty, it becomes one which illustrates and encourages something very like it. (In the former case, generosity to the poor, in the latter simple love for Jesus – though admittedly it is the love of a penitent sinner seeking forgiveness, so that more is involved than pure ethics.)

Other New Testament writings too, in which a slackening

of the urgency of Christ's return is apparent, show a resurgence of firm ethical assertion. The Pastoral Epistles (p. 63) and the Epistle of James (p. 66 in particular, are works for which ethics are an area of comparatively independent and self-sufficient concern.

3. *The example of God and of Jesus.* New Testament writers enjoin the following of certain lines of conduct or the acquiring of certain qualities, not on the grounds of their intrinsic worth or rightness, but on the grounds that they are characteristics of God or of Jesus and are therefore to be imitated as part of a life of discipleship. I Corinthians xi, 1 is the most general statement of this principle. Paul also applies it to specific qualities: to generosity (II Corinthians viii, 9); and to humility (Philippians ii, 3–11). So does I Peter in the matter of the patient endurance of suffering and persecution (ii, 18–25). So too does the Gospel of John in the matter of sacrificial service (xiii, 15; cf. Luke xxii, 24–7). The portrayal of Jesus throughout the Gospel of Luke shows him as one who displayed exemplary love and sacrificial kindness, and who moved sinners to repentance and drew outcasts to his side (e.g. iv, 18ff.; xv; xix, 1–10). And in the Acts of the Apostles, his followers are shown following his example in their works of power and charity (e.g. iii, 1ff.; ix, 36ff.), and in their bearing in the face of suffering (vi, 8ff.; vi, 54ff.).

A moral principle may be seen as grounded not in the behaviour of Jesus but rather in the pattern of his God-given work. Thus, according to Ephesians v, 22ff., the true model for the relationship between husband and wife is to be found in that between Christ and his Church, a bond characterized by loving care on the one side and obedient submission on the other.

Where this mode of reasoning operates, and to the degree

that it operates, ethics lose their autonomy, and conduct is established on a basis other than those of intrinsic values or social desirability.

4. *The divine command*. Not only the example but also the command of God may authenticate lines of behaviour. In the Bible, God's injunctions to men, especially when cast in the prophetic mould ('Thus saith the Lord'), always carry a strong sense of judgement pronounced on man's own efforts. God's ethics stand over against man's ethics and evaluate them. Moreover God commands as seems best to him and not in accordance with norms to which he is bound. This sense of God's moral authority is appropriated to Jesus: for example, Matthew v, 21–48; John xiii, 34. Once more, in so far as it is the external word which is authoritative because of the status of him who utters it, ethics has lost its own independent power, and assertion has replaced rational moral argument. Jesus' 'I say unto you' invites no discussion, uses no logically grounded persuasion. It simply commands obedience.

At first sight there are similarities between this way of authorizing moral imperatives and the way described on p. 6 as one of the two conditions under which ethics are rendered wholly or virtually autonomous. In both cases, God is the authorizer; in both cases a comprehensive scheme for conduct is made available. Yet clearly, there are decisive differences. First, there is in this strand of biblical ethics an essential and pervasive sense of the numinous: it is the holy God who commands by virtue of his deity. Second, the content of what is commanded is secondary in importance to the mere fact that it is commanded. In Matthew v, 21–48, the reader is more deeply impressed by the reiterated 'I say unto you' than by any possible coherent pattern in the conduct which is enjoined. It is for man to receive God's commands, not to reach the satisfaction of possessing a logically consistent code of behaviour.

5. *Justification by faith.* The terminology belongs to Paul, but he shares the general idea which it represents with other New Testament writers. In varying ways, they present the fruit of Christ's work as owing all to God's gracious initiative and nothing to man's earning. Even the Gospel of Matthew, which sets more store than any other major New Testament writing by the punctilious observance of a detailed moral code, clearly sees this as dependent upon Jesus, who summons men to repentance, offers them forgiveness and welcomes them into close relationship with himself (vi, 25–34; xi, 28–30). Men are to aspire to a righteousness greater than that of the scribes and Pharisees (v, 20; xxiii, 2f.), but while this is a condition of entry into the kingdom, it can only be followed once the call of Jesus has been accepted (iv, 17; xxi, 31f.) and life is lived under his aegis (xxviii, 20).

The fact that Matthew, with strong inclinations pressing him towards a legalistic morality, adopts this overall pattern indicates how inescapable it was in the early Church. The facts about Jesus compelled it. In Paul, it finds classical expression and is thoroughly explored. Moral commands have their place as rules for living (Rom. xiii, 8–10), but success in keeping them is not the basis for acceptance by God. That rests solely on faith in Christ and in what God has done through him (Rom. v, 1–5; x, 4–13). John's Gospel makes the same point in other terms, e.g. xv, 1–5, 16.

This emphasis on God's indispensable initiative in the work of man's salvation seems to reduce the importance of moral striving and of independent moral argument; for a central motive in the moral struggle, which gives it bite and seriousness, has apparently been removed: that is, the belief that upon success in it a man's eternal future depends. But no New Testament writer draws that conclusion – except the writer of the Epistle of James, and then only in mis-understanding Paul (ii, 14–26)! Paul himself is clear that men will be judged by their works at the End (I Cor. iii, 13; iv, 5; II Cor. v, 10). There is no hint of treating the moral life as trivial. It is a question of the right appreciation of its role. Essential for the attainment of final salvation, obedience to God's fundamental commands is nevertheless futile and harmful if a man believes that by it he can command God's approval. No man can earn acceptance by God but must receive it gladly as a gift at his hands. That for Paul is the miracle of grace which constitutes the gospel. And as far as it goes, it takes not the seriousness but rather the all-too-common self-concern out of the moral struggle. Ethics have their place within and not outside the redemptive provi-dence of God as he reconciles man to himself in Christ.

However, if we look at it more generally, that religious outlook which manifests itself in Paul in the language of justification by faith is part of a wider spiritual movement of the period – one which generally went hand in hand with that pessimism about the physical universe which we exam-ined earlier (pp. 8–9), and which was its subjective counter-part. This was a passionate desire for salvation and concern with all possible means to its attainment. As salvation was not to be found in the life and activity of this world but only by escape into a wholly mystical present or an otherworldly future, ethics lost their force and significance. God held the initiative, only God could act in this cause; why then should man concern himself with duties dictated solely by his bodily existence? In the mystery cults this reaction appeared in its purest form. 'None of them developed a code of ethics for daily living in addition to regulations for cultic purity ... It goes without saying that other forms of irrational aspiration after salvation and security – such as astrology among the upper classes and magic among the lower classes – also had no ethical norms for daily living.'[3]

How far the Christian movement in the early days was infected by antinomianism of this extreme variety it is impossible to say. Matthew had experienced teaching which he had taken in this sense (vii, 21), and Paul's Corinth was not free of a tendency towards it (1 Cor. vi, 12 – taking 'All things are lawful for me' as the assertion of those whom Paul is controverting). Even without the strength of the surrounding religious atmosphere, the fervour of a new movement can as easily tend this way as in the direction of strict moralism. Among the New Testament writers themselves the primary concern for salvation, given by God, does not have these drastic effects. Nevertheless, it is a force which counteracts the self-sufficiency of ethics as man's proper sphere of purpose and endeavour, and sometimes the argument is on the razor's edge (Rom. iii, 31).

All these forces, which were at work in the religious environment from which the New Testament came, threaten the autonomy of ethics; or, to make the same point in a less belligerently ethical way, they reduce the role of ethics as an independent and all-sufficient concern for man as he reflects on his aims and the conduct of his life. In a variety of ways, all these pressures either make ethics depend upon another religious principle or even (in the extreme case of the gnostic tendency) abolish the validity and worthwhileness of morals as a serious human interest.

This is not their only effect. Some of them, and especially those which are most influential in the New Testament, tend to alter the relative esteem given to particular moral qualities. The virtues of Aristotle's *Ethics* and *Politics* (justice,

3. A. Dihle in H. J. Schultz (ed.), *Jesus in His Time* (London, 1971), p. 13.

temperance, fortitude and prudence) were all qualities valuable for building and improving social and civic life. They relate to purely this-worldly conditions and demands. In the New Testament a quite different set of qualities comes to the fore; lowliness, meekness, long-suffering, gentleness – not at all the virtues by which purposeful and practical social life is built up. Some of these qualities are visibly transpositions into another key of virtues traditionally esteemed: modesty turns into self-denial, dutiful almsgiving into sacrificial generosity. And in the tightly-knit christian body, with its strong dependence on and loyalty to Christ, the duty of fostering the cohesion of the community is intensified: it becomes, in its new form, a major strand in the meaning given to love (e.g. in John's Gospel, cf. p. 36, and Col. iii, 14). Even simple neighbourliness takes on a new meaning: 'whoever gives you a cup of water, *because you are followers of Christ*, will by no means lose his reward' (Mark ix, 41).[4] It is not that the social virtues have no place in the New Testament (cf. p. 64, but rather that they now rank firmly below other qualities and are less closely related to the writers' central concerns. (See I Cor. xiii; II Cor. xii, 5; Phil. ii, 1–11; Rom. v, 3f.; Eph. iv, 1f.)

These newly valued qualities occupy their place because of a new focus of interest. They spring not from social needs but from a sense of man's place in relation to a powerful but gracious God. Where God has all initiative and holds all rights, man is called to abandon his pride; where God has shown himself generous to the point of the cross, man is called to imitate him and to adopt a new scale of values. Paul's giving of prominence to the trio, faith, hope and love, illustrates the point. These terms are complex. Their reference is wider than the narrowly ethical sphere. They do not

4. Normally biblical quotations are from the Revised Standard Version, but here I depart from it.

simply recommend lines of conduct. They are also ways of characterizing the Christian's response to God and his neighbour. They relate to a man's sense of the destiny before him, the aims to which he devotes his whole self.

For Paul in particular, the old virtues and duties were not only to be transcended but were condemned as the occasion of pride. They sprang from man's selfish concern with his own fulfilment and deliberately aimed at achievement that would redound to man's own credit, thus impeding the centring of his attention and allegiance upon God (Rom. iv, 2f.; I Cor. i, 28ff.; iv, 7).

We have examined the leading elements in the ethical attitudes and injunctions of the New Testament writers. In their books we have already seen evidence of a wide range of concepts and emphases. Some of them are part and parcel of the contemporary climate of thought, whether inside or outside Judaism. But some find new modes of expression or appear now in new associations with each other. These new modes derive from the new conditions created by faith in Jesus. Thus, Jesus himself speaks with God-like authority on moral questions (cf. p. 14); and Jesus' life and death are seen as the decisive crisis in the world's history, creating the need for emergency measures in ethical as in other matters (cf. p. 10). We are witnessing here a struggle to discover new categories of thought and speech. In the central New Testament writers, especially Paul and John, the creative process is at its most intense. Others are less enterprising and tend simply to incorporate stock attitudes and tenets. Even Paul is capable of taking over conventional lists of duties and of virtues and vices (e.g. Col. iii, 5–iv, 1).

Theology always threatens the autonomy of ethics. God's appearance always challenges man's own values and aspirations. Conversely, man will only turn to his own moral values when and in so far as he feels either that God is removed from the immediate scene or that God is not vitally concerned with a particular area of behaviour. Thus, in those New Testament writings where the expectation of the return of Christ has lost its urgency and the End is relatively distant, there is a revival of interest in the qualities esteemed in traditional social ethics and in the moral problems of ordinary life. It is not that the religious forces which impinge upon the autonomy of ethics cease to exert themselves; they simply lose some of their power. This is notably true of the Gospels of Matthew and Luke, but to some extent it is true of all the gospels – if it is the case that the very writing of such books meant that Christ's return was now thought of as a relatively distant event (but see p. 45). In the Gospel of Matthew, the fact that the teaching of Jesus occupies so much of the book is itself evidence that the Church is to reckon on a period of life in the conditions of the present age before the Lord returns at its end (xxv, 31; xxviii, 20). For this writer it is of the greatest importance that Christians should know precisely how to regulate the details of their lives. They are given guidance on divorce (v, 32 and xix, 3–9), on celibacy (xix, 10–12), on possessions (xix, 16–30), on internal quarrels in the Church (xviii, 15ff.), among other matters.

In the case of the Gospel of Luke, the virtues of pity for the poor and outcast and generosity in giving alms receive pride of place (x, 30–7; xix, 8; cf. Acts iv, 32–y, 11), both of them virtues which sweeten and establish life in society. In its general standpoint, neither of these gospels reflects an emergency situation where departures from customary behaviour may be demanded (though see Luke xiv, 26).

Similarly, where a writer feels that a particular area of conduct is outside the range of God's immediate concern, worldly ethics reassert themselves. Thus Paul is clear that in Christ human distinctions of race, social status and sex are transcended: his belief in Christ as the new Adam leads directly to this conclusion. But this does not prevent his uncritical acceptance of slavery as a social institution (cf. Col. iii, 22–iv, 1; I Cor. vii, 20 ff.). In certain respects–those important to Paul – it is transcended, but the institution itself goes unquestioned. No doubt this is partly because the End is near, and partly because a major social revolution is a cause beyond the scope of the minute Christian body. But Paul does not always show himself restricted by this consideration (cf. I Cor. vi, 1ff.). It is rather that his theological convictions do not lead to any but conventional results on this particular question. In any case, full consistency is a quality we must not demand in the novel circumstances to which Paul was striving to give conceptual as well as practical expression.

In making our analysis, we have written as if a notional autonomous ethical system suffered violence from a number of external forces to produce the ethics which the New Testament portrays. This approach was convenient for the sake of clarity but we should do wrong to leave the impression that the matter can only be considered at this theoretical level. In the world of the first century A.D. autonomous ethics were a reality. A universalized (and therefore partly individualized) version of the earlier civic ethics was common currency among the educated classes of the Mediterranean world. By this period it owed most to Stoicism for its formal aspects, but this widespread morality was in fact an amalgam of a number of philosophical systems and was most generally propagated at the level of practical counsel rather than high philosophy. It was an ethic of human brotherhood and self-fulfilment, and resulted, at its best, in a spirit that was often humane and tolerant. Certainly it was, left to itself, tolerant in religion, partly because it was so divorced from all specific religious patterns: it stood on its own ground, as a recipe for the moral life, and so was indifferent to the cultic sphere and the quest for salvation. Christians have often underestimated the significance of this ethic in facilitating the spread of Christianity. Persecution struck the Church only fitfully and locally – until the great final persecutions of the third and early fourth centuries; and it was occasioned largely by Christianity's intolerance, offending against the widely endorsed moral instinct of the time. Yet it was the religious toleration favoured by educated opinion which provided a milieu in which the gospel could spread. Men were open to a wide spectrum of religious conviction and practice and were reluctant to stamp out views with which they were themselves not sympathetic.

On the other hand, while Christianity, like Judaism before it, was intolerant and formally uncompromising, it continually absorbed features from the surrounding cultures. This was not simply a matter of using contemporary idioms in which to clothe its distinctive message. There were also elements which had no necessary relation with the christian faith and which the Church had, as it were, no need to take into its system: they came into Christianity because they were an accepted part of the scene, and while some cohered well enough with it, others were at variance with its central message and were evidence of failure to see its implications. This absorption was so striking that, in describing a somewhat later period, it is possible to speak of 'the conversion of Christianity' (Peter Brown, op. cit., pp. 82ff.). The roots of it are already to be found in the New Testament, and, as we have seen, they include elements taken over from pagan ethics. There is the acceptance of the *status quo* in government and of social institutions like slavery and the subordination of women – despite profound innovations concerning these matters at the level of theology (cf. p. 26). There is the favour given to certain moral qualities that were admired at that time, in passages like Philippians i, 9; iv, 8, 11f.[5] There are the conventional lists of virtues and vices, much the same as those found in contemporary pagan and hellenistic jewish literature (e.g. I Cor. vi, 9; Col. iii, 5–12).[6] By these means, bridges were being built from the start which helped to make Christianity intelligible and acceptable; in them lay the seeds both of the adaptability which enabled the Church to speak to the late Roman world and of the mediocrity which was so often to be its price.[7]

In this situation, Christianity began its life. In certain crucial respects it continued a tradition which Judaism had already introduced within the world of the Roman Empire – that of a religion which was indissolubly linked with an ethic and, whatever was the case on the periphery, could at its heart compromise on neither. In one way or another, belief about God was the source of principles of conduct. That does not mean (as we have already seen) that all Christians – any more than all Jews, for that matter – linked the two in the same way. Nor does it mean that Christianity linked the two in the same way as Judaism. The two faiths were exposed to many of the same pressures, and formed many similar patterns of thought, but Christianity nevertheless brought its own new and special insights. Our inquiry must now seek to discover what was the range of patterns in early christian ethical thinking and how much these owed to the creative initiative of Jesus himself.

But first, to end this introductory chapter, let us take the discussion in one more direction. We have linked our analysis to the circumstances of the period in which the

5. Cf. J. L. Houlden, *Paul's Letters from Prison* (Penguin, 1970), pp. 56, 109, 113.

6. Cf. W. L. Knox, *Some Hellenistic Elements in Primitive Christianity* (London, 1944), p. 5; J. L. Houlden, op. cit., p. 204.

7. See F. C. Grant, *Roman Hellenism and the New Testament* (Edinburgh and London, 1962), pp. 91f.

New Testament was written, thus bedding it more firmly into history. We may equally well free it from all particular historical settings and note that most of the forces which we have discovered at work in the New Testament can be found in one form or another wherever ethics and metaphysics coexist. As far as our own society is concerned, self-contained ethical argument may, it is true, be more common than in more religious societies, but it by no means holds the floor, and the familiar range of concepts still appears. Examples abound. The orthodox Marxist recognizes a pressure comparable to that of apocalyptic, bringing about the abrogation of everyday ethical norms. The Sartrean existentialist knows that sense of life's vacuity which moved the Gnostics. Followers of many kinds of mysticism know what it is to experience salvation by the gift of Another's hand rather than as the reward for their own striving. Every political hero-worshipper sees ethics in terms of the imitation of his model. If at first sight the world of the first century seems foreign, a closer look reveals sufficient familiar landmarks.

What is noteworthy is that within the christian Church several of these pressures have lost their strength, and often we have nothing very powerful to correspond with them, even if we retain the language that once carried their force. Our present-day christian ethics are in practice much more autonomous, and much more apt to be argued (if not on a simple appeal to Scripture) on grounds of social or individual utility, than the ethics of the New Testament. They embody values esteemed in the New Testament, but the values *feel* different. They are not now set in the midst of the tensions that pulled at them in the first churches, and if they are still robust, the robustness is of another sort. This in itself should give pause to those inclined to look to the New Testament for *direct* guidance.

2. The Writers

(i) PAUL

PAUL was the first Christian to express himself in writing that has survived, probably the first to express himself in writing at all on a significant scale. He was the first christian writer to give his mind to ethical problems. In this medium he was a pioneer. His mode of expression was the epistle, a semi-formal, semi-public letter, designed for the edification and instruction of a congregation. Such a document demands, in most cases, less precise formulation than the treatise, but more care than the spoken word. Therefore in so far as Paul was a pioneer in setting things down with pen and ink, he was necessarily striving to capture in words ideas and insights that had not so far had to meet this demanding treatment. It is not surprising that he displays no single pattern of thought, but tries out first one pattern and then another. Nor is it surprising that some elements are left over, not integrated with the main structures of his thought. His work is a triumph of creative expression, but its very dynamism left bits of it racing breathlessly behind the main body.

His ethics were mainly determined by his theology. Yet sometimes he fell back on standard judgements. They come through from the contemporary world into his writing, quite unaffected by his belief in the God known through Jesus. For example, he voices no hint of objection to slavery in itself, and in this respect falls below the humane ideals of Stoics of his time like Seneca. In the Epistle to Philemon he seeks the manumission of Onesimus but in the Epistle to the Colossians, where he addresses partially the same audience, he carefully balances this request by stating the

general duty of slaves to be submissive to their masters. One
of his finest and most translucent pieces of teaching is to
proclaim the equality of all believers in Christ – whether
they are Jews or Gentiles, slaves or free men (Gal. iii, 28; I
Cor. xii, 13) – but he shows no hint (is it only because the
End is near; and because in any case Christians are hardly a
significant political force?) of seeing his words as leading to
action. Would a christian slave necessarily have been content with Paul to leave the matter on this exalted plane?

Still, the striking thing about Paul's ethics is the way that
he so often and so sharply brought this central conviction
about Christ to bear upon the solution of moral problems
with which his congregations faced him. In reply to the
church at Corinth, he could easily have fallen back upon
flat, unreasoned prohibition when called upon to deal with
sexual immorality. In fact he appeals straight to the Christian's intimate association with Christ – which renders such
conduct not 'wrong' so much as treacherous or adulterous
(I Cor. vi, 12ff.). He enjoins virtues not as inherently commendable but as following from possession of the Spirit (Gal.
v, 22). He urges generosity and humility not because they
are desirable as virtues but because they are attributes of
Christ in his saving act for men (II Cor. viii, 9; Phil. ii,
1–11). Humility and mutual love are duties which follow
straight from membership in Christ's body, the Church: cf.
the logic of Romans xii, 3, 4 and 9, and xv, 1.

Above all, the moral impulse finds its deepest source in
Christ's death, which for Paul operates at a level more profound than that of inspiration: baptism 'into Christ' brings
about the destruction of the believer's orientation to sin. It is
a wholesale acceptance of Christ's cross – and a dedication
to the self-giving that is consistent with it (Rom. vi, 6–8; Gal.
v, 24).

We have already (pp. 11f.) had occasion to note the presence of contrary tendencies in Paul's moral teaching. In relation to accepted elementary duties and practices, he can say on the one hand 'you must work' but on the other 'you had better not marry'; in relation to political authorities 'you must not go to law with one another' but 'you must pay your taxes'. Is this *mere* contradiction? Does it illustrate our point that Paul has not fully unified his thought? In these cases another solution applies, and its root lies in Paul's eschatology.

To put it simply: viewing God's action in Christ as crucial for man and the universe, Paul sees the New Age, to which in conventional jewish apocalyptic the End of this age would lead, as in a sense already established (I Cor. x, 11). Its marks – the outpouring of the Spirit, the defeat and subordination of the spiritual powers of the cosmos, and the enjoyment of life seen as the fruit of Resurrection – were already discernible (Rom. v, 5; Col. i, 15–20; Rom. vi, 11). And within the christian community, conscious of living already in the last days, intellectual and social values were already being reversed. The world's foolishness is God's wisdom, and the world's nobodies are God's great ones (I Cor. i, 25f.). Moral qualities, love above all, are described – and their manifestation expected – as the outcome of the Spirit's power: cf. Galatians v, 22, and the movement from the account of the Spirit's gifts in I Corinthians xii, to their ethical consequence in ch. xiii.

Yet it was not so *tout court*. What had begun fell far short of final accomplishment. So naturally Paul emphasizes now one side of the matter, now the other, as circumstances dictate.[1] God's great act is already in train, although its consummation lies in the future.

1. See C. F. D. Moule, 'The Influence of Circumstances on the Use of Eschatological Terms', *Journal of Theological Studies*, Vol. 15 (1964), pp. 1ff.

This dual perspective was inevitable, given the history-based orientation which was fundamental to Paul the Jew. He could not help expressing the meaning of Christ by reference to the End, using the images and concepts associated with it. The dual perspective affected Paul's ethics in two ways. In the first place, it led to his producing a number of apparently paradoxical statements, whereby a state of affairs, appropriate to God's completed work, is said to be already enjoyed by Christians; then conduct appropriate to that state of affairs is immediately enjoined. Such exhortation would surely be superfluous if the consummation really had occurred, for the conduct in question would have been established. (See Gal. v, 25; Col. iii, 1; iii, 3, 5 – 'you died' then 'put to death'.)

In the second place, this fundamental perspective of Paul's led to the inconsistent moral judgements which we observed. Sometimes he saw the moral obligations of this present age as so close to being superseded that they could already be thrown to the winds; sometimes he saw these obligations as to be upheld as long as that age persisted. On some of these questions, Paul's decision might have gone either way, according to which side of the matter was uppermost in his thoughts. On marriage, it is possible that we can even discern a change of mind. J. C. Hurd, in *The Origin of I Corinthians* (London, 1965), set out to show that on this and a number of other issues Paul backed down from an original fervent asceticism to a more conventional position. A first reading of I Corinthians vii usually gives the impression that Paul is urging abstention from marriage and from sexual relations within marriage, in view of the coming End (vii, 1–9, 25ff.); but his prohibition is far from absolute (verses 9, 28), and it may be that in this chapter we witness Paul's movement from the one emphasis to the other, in the light of changed pastoral circumstances (perhaps the deleterious effects of the ascetic policy) and the dawning of a sense that the End would be delayed. He now sought to modify his earlier teaching.

This same duality affects not only Paul's moral judgements but also moral motives. Thus, when he looks towards the End, Paul forbids vices on the grounds that they are against God's law and can be expected to produce an adverse verdict in the Judgement which he will then deliver (II Cor. v, 10). Similarly, he urges his readers to strive for virtuous conduct because the End is nearer than when they first believed (Rom. xiii, 11ff.). But when he has in mind the state of affairs newly established through Christ, they are forbidden on the grounds of their incompatibility with life in relation to him (I Cor. vi, 15; II Cor. v, 17; vi, 14f.). Sexual sin is forbidden on both grounds; indeed it heads Paul's lists of vices (e.g. Rom. i, 24–31; Gal. v, 19f.; Col. iii, 5f.; I Thess. iv, 3f.). In terms of the second line of argument, this giving of priority to sexual immorality is not purely formal or conventional. Peculiarly and radically such behaviour offends against a Christian's attachment to Christ, which involves the allegiance of his whole person. In the passage in which this thought is developed (I Cor. vi, 14ff.), Paul does not go so far as to exclude the marriage relationship – he talks only of fornication – but the logic of his argument could well have led him to do so (verse 16). Union with Christ is described in the most exclusive terms. In the next chapter, he does recommend celibacy, but on the basis of arguments that are, in terms of their intrinsic power to compel, less striking. He enjoins it partly because of the coming End and partly out of loyalty to Christ, which might be taken as a weaker version of the argument in vi, 14ff. (It is worth noting that in Matthew xix, 12 celibacy is envisaged 'for the sake of the kingdom of heaven' an expression which most probably means 'because the conditions of Church life demand it', an argument of a quite different character from those employed by Paul.) In I Thessalonians iv, 3ff., sexual immorality is again condemned for a reason deriving from positive christian insight: it is the very antithesis of love of the brethren which Paul goes on to urge. The false use of the affections excludes the true.

In terms of Paul's forensic imagery, we may state this duality thus: the Christian is justified – but he is not thereby exempt from the coming assize of God. And on the basis of either assertion, Paul can dissuade from evil conduct.

Paul is not wholly uniform in his view of the moral stance which is to be dominant in the life of the Christian; though his approaches converge. When he has the present in view, then life in Christ dominates the scene, and freedom is the keynote, especially freedom from the Law. Though pastoral expediency, and in one case at any rate the inherent demands of the Christian's solidarity with Christ (I Cor. vi, 14–20), enter in as limiting factors, he still does not reject the Corinthians' slogan: 'All things are lawful' (I Cor. vi, 12; x, 23; cf. ix, 19–22). When the coming judgement is before his mind, he presents moral life in terms of the shunning of specified vices, though he is mostly confident that Christians' lives will be free from them (I Cor. vi, 9; Col. iii, 4ff.), for their new status – justification and life in Christ – confers protection. The logic of this pair of converging lines deserves more precise statement. When Paul considers the idea of lawfulness in the context of the status already conferred upon the Christian, then freedom is the keynote (Gal. v, 1) and 'all things are lawful' (though limitations may arise as a result of other considerations, such as expediency, and the new life itself gives rise to moral demands); but when he takes the long-term view, then the idea of lawfulness in effect reasserts itself, and lists of forbidden kinds of behaviour are supplied. He can even refer bluntly to the 'law of

Christ' (Gal. vi, 2), though the exact sense (i.e. how far it is ironic or how far *law* means something almost as general as *rule*) is not wholly clear. Once more the two perspectives bring about different lines of ethical argument. Sometimes they can be brought into close harmony, e.g. I Thessalonians v, 8–10: 'since we belong to the day, let us be sober . . . For God has not destined us for wrath but to obtain salvation.'

When it comes to specific moral qualities, love (*agapē*) is pre-eminent (I Cor. xiii, 13; Rom. xiii, 9; Gal. v, 22). In Galatians v, 6, Paul shows why this is so, in terms of his dominant theological pattern. What 'avails' (i.e. for attaining the new relationship with God) is 'faith working through love'. The two concepts come together because they are two sides of the same orientation of a man. Faith denotes the attitude of openness or simple trust on the basis of which alone he can relate truly to God. Love denotes the generous self-giving which flows from it. Faith is a disposition of the whole person, love the moral impulse to which it gives rise; for to respond to God's love in simple trust must impel a man to be open to his neighbours' needs. Open self-giving must characterize a man in both dimensions – towards God and towards others. Not that this correlation is the only, or even the main, line of argument to which Paul appeals. It seems to lie at the heart of his position, but there are also simpler ways of commending love as the crowning virtue. It is the quality which chiefly characterized Christ (Gal. ii, 20), and Paul enjoins the imitation of Christ (I Cor. xi, 1).

The diversity in Paul's modes of expression in ethical matters was brought about, as we have seen, by the nature of his theological task. Using his existing jewish eschatological assumptions, he had to make intelligible the decisive nature of God's act in Christ. The prime result of that act, as far as Paul was concerned, was not to produce a new moral imperative but rather a new state of life: that of reconciliation with God (Rom. v, 1–5; II Cor. v, 16–19). Meanwhile, while this age continues, that life is marked by sufferings and privations like those endured by Christ and closely related to his. By sharing Christ's fate, the Christian most clearly fulfils his calling (II Cor. iv, 7ff.; xii, 7ff.; Col. i, 24). It is in this setting of suffering endured, with the assurance of coming glory (Rom. viii, 15–17), that the ethical questions are commented upon and instruction given. Paul's solutions vary in content and motivation simply because this state of life admits of no single standpoint. He veers from making provision for the realities of life in this world to abandoning the present world-order as no longer worth consideration by those who are 'in Christ' – and then back again. In Colossians iii, 18–iv, 6, there is nothing necessarily or exclusively christian in the logic or the content of Paul's words: Jews and pagans alike would have agreed with him; yet elsewhere, for example in I Corinthians vii, 29–31, he abandons relationships that belong to life within the world, and in I Corinthians xiii wholly transcends its serviceable, practical morality. This represents such a different attitude that some scholars find it hard to believe (not for this reason alone) that the epistle to the Colossians is Paul's work.

Paul's attitude to the Law (whether the jewish Law or law in a more general sense) is less relevant to the question of his ethics than would appear at first sight. His central concern with law as a problem (to say the least) for man, as seen particularly in Romans i–viii and Galatians iii–iv, belongs less in the sphere of ethics than in that of man's whole status in relationship to God. For Paul, law is a theological before it is a moral category. It is concerned first with the question, 'How can I truly relate to God?' and only then with, 'How ought I to behave?' Similarly, sin is a religious category before it is a moral category. It is a force which beguiles and enslaves man (Rom. vii), not simply wrongdoing.

Paul's complaint against law is not that it is misleading as a moral guide – as such he hardly considers it in his central theological argument (though see Romans vii, 12) – but rather that it fails to enable man to satisfy his overriding need: acceptance with God. In this it is even a positive hindrance, for man in search of this acceptance commits the error of attributing value to his moral actions (Gal. ii, 15–iii, 5). Ethics come up for consideration not in relation to this need, but later, when it has been filled (by faith in Christ). Then indeed the moral law comes into its own (Rom. xiii, 8–10). Love bears the palm, as we have seen, but some of the Ten Commandments are quoted and endorsed. How Paul distinguished between elements in the jewish Law which were binding on Christians and elements which were not he never tells, but the natural supposition is that the ceremonial law was frankly jettisoned. This was partly because of the equal acceptance of Gentiles into the Church alongside Jews, partly because its provisions (unlike love of the neighbour) did not spring naturally from the pattern of life in Christ, partly also because only with danger did its observance avoid the attempt to establish merit *vis à vis* God.

Nevertheless, Paul's attitude to the Law, even as a theological category, is not one of sheer hostile confrontation. Rather, he sees the Law as now superseded; and, what is more, for him this change is provided for in the Law itself – rightly understood. It has within it the grounds for its own retirement from the scene of man's dealings with God. Thus, the Law itself contains the principle of justification on the basis of faith (cf. Rom. iv, 1–12), and by its cursing of those who suffer death by hanging it is the instrument of its own end, inasmuch as God's Son has come under its ban and thus (so Paul seems to be saying) made this death a means of blessing (Gal. iii, 13).

If Paul can appeal to the Law for the basis of the doctrine

that its day is now past (Gal. iii, 23f.), he can also appeal to it on occasion as an authority for moral or ecclesiastical custom. Thus, the right of the apostle to be maintained by his flock is justified, in rabbinic manner, by reference to Deuteronomy xxv, 4 (I Cor. ix, 9), and the duty of women to have their heads covered in meetings of the congregation is backed by reference to the Creation story (I Cor. xi, 8f., cf. Gen. ii, 21ff. and M. D. Hooker, *New Testament Studies*, 10, 1964). Even on matters like these, which are in a category quite different from the fundamental moral law of the Decalogue, Paul can still look to the Law for a ruling; though in the latter case, he appeals also to two other principles, natural common sense (I Cor. xi, 14f.) and church custom (I Cor. xi, 16). In other words, as Paul's ethics spread out towards the edges, especially when he turns to questions on which it would be hard to see the bearing of central beliefs and where perhaps the best a man can do is to rationalize his prejudices or intuitive convictions, he makes use of principles which are not easily worked into the central logic of his teaching. (Lofty as the expression of it is, the justification of women's subordination to men in marriage on the basis of Christ's relationship with the Church in Ephesians v, 22ff. needs to be seen in this light.)

Paul's ethics do not start from anything which man can offer to God by way of virtuous conduct, but from what God has done for man. The standard ethical notions of 'the good', of virtue and of duty play hardly any part; rather goodness springs from grace and life in the body of Christ. Only if a man ceases to be a slave to morality and becomes the slave of Christ (I Cor. vii, 21f.) can the spirit enable him to live in freedom and love.

(ii) JOHN

The Fourth Gospel is the outstanding example in the New Testament of a writing which accords a minimal role to autonomous ethics. The world, in the sense of a society of flesh and blood, posing moral problems for man and providing the scene for the success or failure of his ideals, is absent from this work. 'The world' for John is a totality: which God loves and desires to save; to which he sends his Son for salvation and not judgement (iii, 16f.), though the world, inexorably, brings judgement on itself (xii, 31). He will not take his own out of the world; nevertheless, like the Son they are aliens there (xvii, 14ff.), and are neither promised joy nor given a task in it. At the crisis, Jesus does not pray for the world, but only for those given to him by God out of the world (xvii, 9). In the trial Jesus stands before Pilate, and there he unmistakably confronts the world. Though there is the hope that the world may 'believe' and 'know' (xvii, 21, 23), the mission (xvii, 18) seems to be an act of confrontation rather than embrace.

It is hard to believe that a work such as this is not to be rightly identified as gnostic in tendency. It is not our concern here to locate the Gospel of John on the thought-map of the early Church, but this absence of interest in the world of everyday events and the movement of external history certainly points towards Gnosticism (cf. p. 8). This does not mean that John shares all the tenets associated with the sects of the second century; demonstrably he does not. It means that in the wide spectrum of New Testament thought he tends in that direction and can usefully be interpreted with that fundamental standpoint in mind. It is not only that by contrast with a writer like Luke he gives no sense of the world of events; not only that when figures like Annas, Caiaphas and Pilate appear, the latter two (Annas' part is small) speak and act only to serve Johannine purposes; not only that 'the world' is a theological category rather than a secular reality; more fundamentally, it is the case with John that though his Jesus comes for the world's salvation, the world is nevertheless the scene of unbelief, and salvation is rescue from it.

It is therefore natural that for John the believer has no duties towards 'the world', but only towards those who like himself are saved from it. The new commandment (xiii, 34f.) is not that the neighbour is to be loved (and notice how widely that was capable of being taken, Luke x, 27ff.; cf. Rom, xiii, 9; Mark xii, 31), still less the enemy (Matt. v, 44; Luke vi, 27), but rather the fellow-Christian. Yet it is unfair to disparage this as a regrettable narrowing of the broad generosity of Paul and the other Gospels. (Who has ever read it thus?) Looked at in John's perspective, it could not be otherwise: his ethics followed straight from his theological convictions. In the world which he saw, a world in which salvation was hard to find, a world in itself the object of near despair, a man's moral duty could only lie within the christian circle, where alone 'meaning' was to be found. Society at large had no moral claims; the question of general obligations simply did not arise. It is not that such obligations are wilfully refused: they do not enter within this writer's purview.

'Love one another' is the *only* moral rule given by John. Three times he refers to 'the commands' (plural) of Jesus (xiv, 15, 21; xv, 10), but never says what they are. We may not assume that he means us to have read the Gospels of Matthew and Luke, where these commands appear in plenty: it is more likely that 'keeping my commands' has the general sense of 'obeying me', 'doing what I say'. He gives no ruling of Jesus on marriage, divorce, property or the state. That which the other writers see as the crown and guiding principle of Jesus' ethical teaching is (with its limitation to 'one another') for John its whole content.

When he expounds that command (xv, 13–17), it is in terms of continuing in the community which Christ has initiated. Behind the duty of love to each other and acting as its source is the mutual love of Christ and the believer. That love found its chief and seminal expression on the cross (xv, 13). When it is once received, it then issues in mutual love among the believers, and they come to be on a level with Christ – his friends (xv, 14). His life and work continue in them. Such is John's analysis in terms of love. But this doctrine of mutuality between Christ and the believer can be expressed by John in terms other than those of love; for example, in terms of self-disclosure (xiv, 21), or mission (xx, 21), or activity (xiv, 12). All these terms are for John ways of stating the central reality – the relationships between Christ and the believer and of the believers among themselves, which reproduce that between Father and Son. In other words, even when he speaks of the command to love and of doing what Jesus commands, John's real concern is not primarily ethical at all. His concern is with the new condition of life conferred on the believer through Christ. In iii, 21, though there is reference to 'deeds', the object of the verb 'to do' is not 'the good' or 'the right', as we might expect (to balance 'evil' in the preceding verse), but 'the truth' – a surprising word in an ethical context, whatever the exact nuance of the word here,[3] but less surprising if 'the truth' is one of John's words for denoting the life and status which Christ confers. The alternative to evil is a way whose meaning transcends the ethical sphere. For John, the

3. Cf. C. H. Dodd, *The Interpretation of the Fourth Gospel* (Cambridge, 1953), pp. 170ff.; S. Aalen in F. L. Cross (ed.), *Studia Evangelica*, Vol. II (Berlin, 1964), pp. 3ff.

all-important thing is for a man to become one with the Son whom the Father has sent.

'Love' is for him, then, primarily, a key term for the bond of the community. We may compare Colossians iii, 14, though Paul is less thoroughgoing in this respect than John, for whom love is almost a synonym for eternal life – a synonym with an ethical flavour.

The First Letter of John, which issues probably from the same circle rather than from the same writer as the Gospel, appears at first sight to have a much more pronounced ethical interest. In terms of sheer space, this impression is correct; but in the end, at the level of belief, the appearance deceives. Like the writer of the Gospel, this writer counts love as the only virtue – at least, he mentions no other (except perhaps purity, iii, 3). Like him, he refers to God's (or Christ's) commandments (ii, 3, 4; iii, 22, 24; v, 2f.) but never tells us what they are.[4] Like him, while not in the least neglecting the moral content of 'love' – he is concerned that his readers should not sin (ii, 1) and regards hatred, love's opposite, as sin *par excellence* (ii, 11) – he sees love as the cement which binds together the life of the christian community. Love is not one moral quality among others; it is the moral expression of walking in the light or living according to the truth or being in fellowship with God (i, 6), and of all the other terms which he uses to describe the new life which has been established through Christ and which he is concerned to strengthen. This intimate link between belief and conduct is explicit in the unique expression of 'his commandment' in iii, 23: that we both believe and love. Love stiffens the christian group, and

4. The impression that he leaves to us is that he means a quite general obedience, such as he can also describe as keeping 'his word' (ii, 5), or doing 'what pleases him' (iii, 22), or doing 'right' (iii, 10) – which he sees as very close to brotherly love.

is a defence against 'the world' – the transient, evil, dark
entity which lies beyond the frontiers of the christian community, where the Antichrist rules (iv, 3). That entity must
receive no love from Christians (ii, 15) and indeed cannot
do so – it is metaphysically impossible. Moreover, the love
within the community derives, as in the Gospel, from God
(iii, 1), and the believer returns it to him as well as sharing
it with the brothers (ii, 5). Indeed, love for the brothers is
the touchstone for the genuineness of love for God (iv, 19–21).

Love seems almost like a huddling together for warmth
and safety in the face of the world. Yet there is also a stern
strength about the moral demand of this writer, and behind
it lies the triumphant conviction that the evil one has
suffered defeat (ii, 12–14). For 'it is the last hour', and the
brothers will not have long to wait before the victory is
complete. Because of the crisis and because Christ's work
has created a total division between the circle of light and
'the world' which lies under the Antichrist's power (v, 19),
there can be no obligation here any more than in the Gospel
to love beyond the bounds of the brotherhood (iii, 14ff.). The
extension of love beyond the Church is then ruled out both
by the nature of the quality itself and by the circumstances
in which the Church lives.

This writing is a prime instance of that pessimism about
the world of ordinary experience which leads people to
abandon serious ethical concern with the problems of everyday life. What place can they have in the interests of those
confronted with the End? This was one only too natural response to the saving act of God in Christ. In terms of our
original analysis, (pp. 8ff.), we see two forces at work, the
world-depreciating and the apocalyptic. Their combination
here has ample parallel in the Judaism of the first century, as
the writings of the Qumran sect testify, in their own idiom
and setting. However, it is important to be precise and not to

overstate the case. Certainly the First Letter of John devalues 'the world', but it would be quite wrong to suppose that he devalues it as far as the gnostic sects were to do, or as far as many of his contemporaries did. He is insistent – against Christians, it seems, who deny it – that Christ came 'in the flesh' (iv, 2), though it is not altogether easy to see why this is so important for him as he gives no rationale. Was it simply 'in his bones', taken for granted, or the effect of the pull of other Christians more 'this-worldly' than himself? Again, there is no strong esoteric flavour about this work, nothing in the way of mysterious names or words, nothing about the need for secrecy about the teaching given. So if we may describe this writing as in some ways gnostic in tendency, that term has to be understood only in a certain sense and with careful qualification. We must not judge the writer by categories appropriate after his time: the Johannine writings are full of contradictions which appear much sharper than they should, if they are evaluated by that misleading, anachronistic method.[5]

It is the last hour and the world is doomed. Only by coming out of its darkness and into the community of light can salvation be assured. What the writer believes is the future of the social fabric and the historical process is left quite unclear. He tells us nothing of the details of the programme which he thinks will ensue, and we cannot assume that the Revelation to John, despite its title, comes from circles close enough to his to give the answer to our question. Rather, the loving brotherhood is an end sufficient to itself, persistent and self-contained, though hope of transfiguration at the End is a spur to present virtue (iii, 2f.). The impression given by the letter is then like that given by the Supper Discourses in the Gospel (ch. xiii–xvii).

5. See S. S. Smalley, 'Diversity and Development in John' (New Testament Studies, Vol. 17, 1971).

The Johannine writings have often been taken as a charter for those convinced of the need to apply the faith to social and political issues. 'The Word was made flesh' (John i, 14) has been taken to signify the sanctification of the whole of the physical, material world, and thereby to decree the Christian's duty to work to make the world worthy to be the dwelling of Christ. Our understanding of both the Gospel and the First Epistle fails to support this view as representing the writers' thought, and indeed even the Prologue of the Gospel can be held to favour the conclusion we have reached through a consideration of the ethical teaching.[6] No New Testament writer has less interest in the sanctifying of ordinary life than these. The pressures to which they respond are far removed from those of the industrial society which gave rise to the interpretation to which we have referred. They write as members of a small enclosed christian group, confident of salvation, sure that the world is reaching its end, convinced indeed that the God who created all things has acted to save but unable to feel that his action works effectively outside the brotherhood of Christ's people. This is not to say that theological principles implicit in these writings may not lead, by a certain route, to applications quite unlike any that the authors could have envisaged; that is another matter. The exegetical point is that they did not formulate those principles with the application we have mentioned anywhere near their minds.

(iii) MARK

If it is right to take paucity of ethical material as *prima facie* evidence of gnostic tendencies (see pp. 8f.), then the Gospel of Mark is a candidate for consideration in this light, not

6. See E. Käsemann, *New Testament Questions of Today* (London, 1969), chapter VI, 'The Structure and Purpose of the Prologue to John's Gospel'.

indeed with the same assurance as in the case of the Fourth Gospel, but still with a degree of confidence. 'Paucity' is a relative term but undeniably the space given by Mark to the ethical teaching of Jesus is small by comparison with the Gospels of Matthew and of Luke. And 'gnostic', as we have seen, is an imprecise term; but it is useful, in a context like this, as an indicator. It can help us to get our bearings, provide a hypothesis for us to confirm or refute. Even if it turns out to be only an Aunt Sally, it is not wholly profitless.

The paucity of ethical material may of course have some explanation quite other than that lack of serious concern with everyday living, which would lead us legitimately to invoke 'gnosticism' as a useful word for describing Mark's theological standpoint. It may be that in a book designed to present the christian proclamation by means of the traditions concerning Jesus' life and death (and this seems a fair statement of his aim, cf. i, 1; 14f.), moral guidance was hardly to the point – it would have been a diversion from the theme. Or else he wrote to complement a known tradition of Jesus' moral teaching; or perhaps to counter those who appealed too strongly to a rabbinic, law-giving Jesus.

The 'gnostic' hypothesis, however, does not rest only on the negative factor of the lack of ethical material. Other considerations arise which both strengthen it and enable the sense of the word as applied to Mark's Gospel to appear more exactly.

The first of these is the esoteric quality which pervades this book. Jesus' baptismal commissioning is a mystery revealed to him alone (i, 10f.). His words are constantly enigmatic and mysterious, above all in the narrative of his Passion, where his every statement, and his silence too, possesses this quality (e.g. vi, 52; viii, 14-17; xiv, 22–5; xv, 5, 34).[7] His parables are to be understood only by initiates (iv,

7. Cf. J. C. Fenton, *Preaching the Cross* (London, 1958); Q. Quesnell, *The Mind of Mark* (Rome, 1969).

11; 33f.). His glory is disclosed only to the inner trio among his disciples, and even they see only dimly (ix, 2ff.); and the knowledge concerning the End is imparted only to the four who were first called (xiii, 3; i, 16—20). His deeds of power, apparently such public acts, are not for the impressing of the crowd (viii, 11f.). His resurrection is a hidden thing, to strike even his followers with unspeakable wonder and fear (xvi, 1–8).

The second consideration is of more direct concern to us. Even the ethical material which Mark includes is for the most part not present as a result of purely ethical interest. Like his miracle stories and his parables, it is a vehicle for conveying two intimately related realities, which are of deeper significance than the material initially suggests. The first reality is the person of Jesus, the mysterious Son of Man sent from God to battle against the powers of evil and 'give his life as a ransom for many' (x, 45). The second reality is the kingdom of God, that immediate and complete sovereignty of God which Jesus embodies and establishes. Moral lessons are taught chiefly as exemplifying and demonstrating these realities. Thus, the sabbath law must give way, not before a set of amended regulations, but before a God who has only one choice when it comes to saving life or destroying it (iii, 4), and before the Son of Man who is the sabbath's lord (ii, 28). Divorce may no longer be tolerated, not because of a new divine decree, but because God created man for life-long marriage – it is at the root of his nature (x, 2f.). Food taboos are abandoned not by a mere alteration of the rules, but because of a wholly different conception of what constitutes uncleanness in the sight of God (vii, 1–23). It is true that a list of forbidden vices is given (vii, 21f.), but these sins are condemned because they strike at man's purity before God, not because they 'break the rules'. What renders the widow's mite so commendable is not her mere generosity, but her self-abandonment in God's cause (xii, 41—4).

There are other cases where this way of looking at apparently ethical passages in Mark is less clearly right. Should we not take the dispute about the tribute (xii, 13–17) as a ruling on the question of the payment of imperial taxes? In that case, it will be not unlike the direction given by Paul in Romans xiii, 1ff. But it has long been suggested[8] that even if this is the evangelist's sense, the passage had another sense at the earlier, oral stage of its existence, and, if authentic, the crucial words ('Render to Caesar the things that are Caesar's, and to God the things that are God's') had a quite different emphasis when they fell from Jesus' lips. Far from being a tidy assigning of two distinct spheres of obligation, thus neatly squashing the opponents, they are an impatient brushing aside of the Pharisees' question, then a thunderous assertion of God's rights, which are total. Only this sense is consistent with Jesus' central and insistent message: that God rules. But if this is so, may it not be that Mark himself included the words with this sense? He, after all, is our first evidence for believing that this was indeed the message of Jesus, and it would be out of character if the shallower rather than the deeper meaning were truly his intention. This story then gives no general ruling about a citizen's duty but an assertion of God's sovereignty which leaves man with every particular decision in this area (when to obey, when to rebel) still to make. Like the other cases we have discussed, an ethical issue is raised only to be settled at the level of theology rather than of ethics. For Mark, the answer to the question, 'What is my duty with regard to X?' is, 'God is sovereign – live under his rule.'

It is the same with the passage in which Jesus gives the two commands (to love God and to love one's neighbour as

8. See, recently, E. Schweizer, *The Good News according to Mark* (London, 1971), p. 244.

oneself) which are greater than all others (xii, 28–34). Here indeed is a provision of moral rules, but the result of even perceiving them is to be 'not far from the kingdom of God'. They are less rules for moral guidance than keys to the realization of God's rule. The same too with the passage about the abuse of Corban (vii, 9–13); for the point is not merely to show the fundamental law of God that lies behind the scribal tradition but to condemn blasphemous worship. It is an attitude to God that is at stake (vii, 6f.).

For this writer then, as for John, it appears that facing and settling moral problems, in the everyday sense, was not a primary concern. He had no eye for casuistry. Unless Mark simply decided, for whatever reason, not to include ethical material in his book, we must conclude that the christian circle to which he belonged did not feel the need of this kind of aid from the tradition about their Lord. In the case of John, it seemed reasonable to look for the explanation of this in his attitude to 'the world'. While not regarding it as the work of evil power or the outcome of cosmic error, as the Gnostics came to do, John tends nevertheless to devalue it. In the case of Mark, there is no trace of this feature, and we must seek another explanation. It is most likely to lie in his eschatology. For Mark, the End, though not immediately to appear (xiii, 7), was not far away. The whole tone of chapter xiii (also ix, 1) makes this unmistakable (especially xiii, 14). The petty persecution which attends the christian mission is itself a sign that the time draws close (xii, 9ff.). Moreover, it is probable that Mark saw the End as already either partly anticipated or else inaugurated in the death of Jesus.[9]

The very existence of Mark's Gospel is often counted a strong argument against the belief that Mark believed in the

9. R. H. Lightfoot, *The Gospel Message of Saint Mark* (Oxford, 1950), pp. 48ff.

nearness of the End: why should he write at such a time? Was not the decline of this belief a potent factor in the very production of 'gospels'? Among so many unknowns, this objection is impossible to counter in the abstract; though it is not too hard to envisage this book, so urgent in tone, being written in the hour of crisis as a tract for the times. The fact remains that Mark must be taken as found and cannot easily be read in any other way. (cf. p. 69.)

In this eschatologically charged atmosphere, it is no surprise that the day-to-day problems of conduct in this world should either cease to be raised or appear in a completely new light. Attitudes are now determined by Jesus, the eschatological emissary of God, and by the presence of the kingdom.

We can then improve upon the generality of our 'gnostic' hypothesis. It deserves to be upheld in so far as esoteric apocalypticism was indeed one element within the welter of religious ideas and attitudes designated by that term. But other elements in the gnostic spectrum are lacking, and Mark's patent shortage of ethical material is primarily to be laid at the door of those features of his theology which we have described.

For him, conduct was determined more by theological factors than by ethical pronouncements, whether in terms of a code or a philosophy. He was not moved by considerations of utility or prudence or by abstract values but by the character and purposes of God. He was not concerned to provide a handbook of morals for the guidance of christian congregations; his wish was that they should sense the overwhelming power and mystery of God and accept his rule. Even his most patently ethical statements are in the end no exception.

(iv) MATTHEW

The account we have given of Mark may carry more conviction when it is set alongside Matthew, who to such a large extent took Mark, and visibly modified what he found. In the matter of ethics, the modifications, often slight in themselves, are the result of profound differences of outlook. The two books, so close in words and structure, are worlds apart as expressions of early christian faith. Before we turn to the ethical teaching itself, then, we must define the distinction between them.

The key is best found in Matthew's last section of all (xxviii, 16–20). There the exalted Jesus, at a final meeting with his disciples, solemnly inaugurates the period of the universal mission, out of which the evangelist writes. That mission, carried out by a Church assured of Jesus' constant presence (xxviii, 20), is of a strongly ethical character. Its aim is to enrol disciples – pupils, after the rabbinic manner – whose discipleship will manifest itself in the observance of Jesus' commands. These are largely contained in the great discourses of Jesus recorded in the earlier part of the Gospel, which are not taken from Mark but found for the first time in this book.

This final section, announcing the strategy which the Church is to follow, effectively divides the life and mission of the Church from the ministry of Jesus. The significance of this is twofold. It takes for granted that the future is long and stable enough to be worth providing for: though the End will certainly come and Christians must await it vigilantly (xxv), it is not expected so soon that a detailed ethical programme is too elaborate for the Church's needs. It means also that the ministry of Jesus with his disciples acquires an exemplary role: they have become the models, drawn from a past already beginning to be idealized, for imitation by the

Christians of the present. So the incomprehension, hostility and treachery which characterize their behaviour according to Mark, are, as far as possible, shaded out or toned down. (Thus, Peter's confession at Caesarea Philippi receives an enconium (Matt. xvi, 17–19). Though the attack on Peter as satanic remains, now in startling and dramatic contrast (Mark viii, 32f; cf. Matt. xvi, 22f.), it is an attack on one whose high and crucial role has been assured beyond all doubt. (Also contrast the disciples' lack of understanding according to Mark viii, 21 with the opposite in Matt. xvi, 11f.)

With Matthew, it is possible to speak of Christianity as a way of life and a path of duty. Jesus is not, as in Mark, the enigmatic Son of Man who is the source of a hard and mysterious way marked by the Cross (e.g. Mark viii, 34; x, 38) so much as the authoritative teacher of clear and strenuous moral lessons, to be carried into practice in fellowship with him and the community which he founded. Many of these lessons are general, but there is nothing haphazard or 'inspirational' about Matthew's conception of christian life. On many of the practical issues which Christians were likely to face in his day, he gives adequate and explicit guidance. Thus, in relation to divorce, the discussion is concerned not, as in Mark, with the purpose of marriage in the providence of God, but with the precise grounds on which divorce may be countenanced (Mark x, 1ff.; cf. Matt. xix, 1ff.). It is a shift from theology to Church law. Not only the teaching of Jesus but incidents in his life are presented so as to give this necessary guidance; for example, xvii, 24–7, concerning the payment of the temple tax.

For Matthew, the christian way is built on an already existing and persisting foundation, the jewish Law. There is no doubt that in his view this remains in force for Christians (v, 17; xxiii, 3, 23). Here we find none of the subtle combining of continuity with discontinuity, acceptance with rejection, which makes Paul so paradoxical and profound in his understanding of the role of Law in God's work for man. Rather, the Law is accepted in principle and largely in content; only, its central moral provisions are intensified by Jesus' authority, and some of its ceremonial features are set in the light of fundamental rules. Jesus brings a greater righteousness, transforming the Law by adding to its rigour (v, 20–48); while love of God and of the neighbour are singled out as commands which do not depreciate so much as provide the basis for the rest (compare Mark xii, 31–33 with Matt. xxii, 40).

Matthew then brings us closer to an ethic which stands in its own right. Of course he presents all as the teaching of Jesus, and his authority is vital to Matthew's scheme of thought. Nevertheless, remove the authorizer from the scene, and this pattern is, despite qualifications (p. 51), not incapable of independent existence; purely as a scheme of ethics it has the makings of self-sufficiency. It is thus unlike the ethics of, for example, the Gospel of John, where love is, as we have seen, closely integrated with the mutual indwelling of Christ and those who belong to him. In Matthew, then, ethics are both more central and more important than in the writers we have so far examined. The End is not so imminent, neither is human society so despaired of as to reduce the need to provide guidance for the moral problems of everyday life. The relationship between Christ and his followers is not expressed in terms of intimate, mystical interaction and indwelling, but in the more external language of obedience and discipleship.

The strength of Matthew's ethical interest is apparent in the frequency with which he turns episodes which in Mark have a theological point into stories where the reasoning and the message are ethical. We have already mentioned the in-

stance of marriage and divorce (see also p. 78). There are
many others. For example, the story of the disciples in the
cornfield (Mark ii, 23–8; Matt. xii, 1–8): Mark reaches a theological conclusion about man's position in relation to the
sabbath as an institution, whereby he is its master and not
its slave; whereas Matthew, by omitting ii, 27 and ampli-
fying and tightening the argument from the Scriptures, turns
it into a justification of a dispensation being granted by
Jesus, who as Son of Man has the authority required for the
case. The general law of sabbath is not impugned. Jesus'
authority is asserted; yet, for good measure, he justifies his
ruling on firm scriptural grounds, for his mission is not to
abolish but to fulfil the Law (v, 17).

Similarly, in the story of the healing of the man with the
withered hand (Mark iii, 1–6; Matt, xii, 9–14), Mark shows
Jesus presenting his attackers with the stark alternatives, 'Is
it lawful to do good or to do harm on the sabbath, to save
life or to kill?' – thus using the presence of the diseased man
to raise issues at a level far deeper than the merely legal. It
would be no answer to Jesus' challenge to reply, 'Let him
wait till the sabbath is over.' God's will is at every moment
for good rather than evil, salvation rather than death.
Matthew omits the stark alternatives, but gives ample argument from Scripture to justify Jesus' healing in this particular case: it is lawful, he maintains, to aid animals in distress
on the sabbath, human beings count for more than beasts,
therefore it is morally and legally justifiable to heal this
man, sabbath though it is. Jesus performs the radical action,
yet the Law remains inviolate and the action is justified on
ethical-cum-legal rather than deeply theological principles.

In the passage concerning the tradition of the elders
(Mark vii, 1–23; Matt. xv, 1–20), which for both evangelists
carries an ethical message, Mark shows God's concern for
man's central moral allegiance by emphasizing that what

matters is the heart. In the process he gives short shrift to the developed scribal tradition whereby the Law was elaborated and applied. On the other hand, Matthew, unwilling to divest the tradition of its authority, confines himself to condemning obvious abuse. His device is to move the section on Corban (Mark vii, 9–12) from after the key quotation from Isaiah xxix, 13 to before it. That quotation, with its sharp attack on the giving of mere lip-service to God (which it identifies with the treatment of human commands as if they were divine), then stands not as a general condemnation of all such hypocrisy (as in Mark) but as a comment on the specific and palpable abuse of Corban. No right-minded man could disagree.

In passages such as these, where Mark is available for comparison, Matthew shows the centrality of his ethical drive. Not that he is legalistic, harsh or cold. For all his concern to provide a comprehensive pattern for christian life, it remains vital for him that this is the gracious gift of a generous and forgiving Lord (vii, 7–11; xxi, 31f.). His scheme is no mere code presented for man to obey independently and in his own strength (xviii, 20). His provisions are often prescriptions for the life of the Kingdom rather than regulations envisaging specific circumstances; for example, the commands not to be anxious (vi, 34) and not to judge (vii, 1–5). And God's reward awaits the faithful disciple (vi, 4, 6, 14; xxiv, 46). This spirit is summed up in the injunctions to seek the greater righteousness (v, 20; vi, 33) and to be perfect (v, 48). We have already pointed to the importance of xxviii, 20: Jesus is with his people for ever. The teaching of Jesus points to this lasting relationship: it is one of gentleness and forgiveness (xi, 28–30; xviii, 14, 23–35), under a God who is wholly to be trusted (vi, 25–34; xiv, 28–31); though discipline, exercised in God's name in the Church, will still be firm and stringent (xviii, 15–18; xxii, 11–14). And for all the width with which he states the command to love (v, 44), Matthew's sympathy does not extend to the Church's pharisaic critics, with whom controversy must have been fierce in the circles to which he belonged (xxiii). It is hard to believe that he envisaged much of a future in God's providence for them, the leading representatives of apostate Israel (xxi, 33–43). What meaning would he have given to the duty to extend love to them?

The life of obedience to Jesus' commands includes not only ethical matters but also the single-minded performance of the duties of piety – prayer, fasting and almsgiving (vi, 1ff.). Life lived faithfully and generously along this path is the sign of membership of the Kingdom of Heaven (xiii, 43) and will in due time bring the glorious reward (xxv, 14–46).[10]

We must add one more refinement to our picture. It concerns the eschatological framework within which Matthew operates. As we have seen, the End is in his view sufficiently distant to enable him to envisage a continuing mission of the Church and to be concerned with its ethical and institutional problems (e.g. xviii, 12ff.). Nevertheless, the final Judgement is constantly before him. Indeed, this writer has more material relating to rewards and punishments than any other evangelist. He offers in vivid if conventional terms both the delights of heaven and the direst torments of hell (xxv, 31–46). He persistently appends the formula: 'there men will weep and gnash their teeth' (viii, 12; xiii, 42, 50; xxii, 13; xxiv, 51) – found nowhere else in the Gospels except once in Luke (xiii, 28). He consistently binds commands and exhortations to promises for the future assize, sometimes giving to sayings which could in themselves

10. See G. Barth, 'Matthew's Understanding of the Law', in G. Bornkamm, G. Barth, and H. J. Held, *Tradition and Interpretation in Matthew* (London, 1963).

easily be read as maxims for present conduct a clear reference to reward or punishment on the Last Day: for example, xvi, 24–6 in the light of xvi, 27; cf. x, 39–42. And compare Matthew xix, 27–30 with Mark x, 28–31, where Matthew omits Mark's reference to the present life of the Church (x, 30), throwing the rewards wholly into the future.

This striking concern of Matthew's with the Judgement, especially in its character as simple requital, need not however lead us to modify our original estimate of his eschatology; it does not mean that after all he sees the End as on the very threshold. Nor need we believe that the many sayings concerned with this theme are included by the evangelist out of faithfulness to the tradition of Jesus' sayings despite their indigestibility from the standpoint of his own, later outlook. Rather, they reflect his love of structure and scheme: the picture must be full and detailed, right to the End – whenever it will come. He shows the same concern with the beginning (his careful genealogy) and in his meticulous treatment of the fulfilment of the prophecy.

Finally, the End is not so far away that it has no effect whatsoever on moral priorities; or it may be rather that the christian community itself, living in expectation of the End and assured of its role on that day, brings about new emphases. At all events, kindness to Christians now becomes a virtue in its own right which will assure reward at the last (x, 42; xxv, 31—46).

Note on the Sermon on the Mount

Classically and popularly, the Sermon on the Mount (Matt. v–vii) has been regarded as the quintessence of the moral teaching of Jesus. In the main, in the pre-critical era, this view rested on the assumption that the Sermon was a record of the veritable words of the Lord, delivered, as the Gospel relates, on a single occasion. Modern criticism nearly always denies the second of these notions and frequently challenges the first. Critics vary greatly in the degree of authenticity they admit in these chapters, depending on their general view of Matthew's use of sources. Those who see him as depending heavily on the tradition find in the Sermon a reliable echo of Jesus' teaching, and, because of the nature of its contents, they continue to locate the heart of Jesus' ethic there; even if, like Jeremias, who sees it as a collection of Jesus' sayings, they show how that ethic rests on doctrinal, 'gospel', foundations. Those who give the evangelist a more creative role find here evidence not so much of Jesus' ethical teaching as of the moral aspect of Matthew's way of holding christian faith, and are not surprised to find it permeated by the beliefs and attitudes to be found throughout his book.

In our account, we have made the simple assumption that, from whatever source he derived it, Matthew subscribed to what he wrote. This assumption, part and parcel of the view of the second kind of critic, need not be held by the first, but he has no need to deny it. Once assume it, and, in a survey such as this – at this point at least – the question of sources and authenticity need not be raised: whatever else it is (such as the teaching of Jesus himself, or the teaching of groups in the early Church), the Sermon on the Mount at least presents the ethics, or part of the ethics, in which Matthew believed. Thus, we have not found ourselves treating it as a special unit, nor have we concentrated our attention upon it. Rather, parts of it have entered, as appropriate, into our presentation of the evangelist's ethics, which colour in a variety of ways his whole pattern of thought.[11]

11. See further the lecture by J. Jeremias, *The Sermon on the Mount* (London, 1961); and the major work, W. D. Davies, *The Setting of the Sermon on the Mount* (Cambridge, 1961), especially chapter VI; and the same author's shorter work *The Sermon on the Mount* (Cambridge, 1966).

(V) LUKE

Like Matthew, Luke provides an example of something closer to autonomous ethics than Paul, John or Mark. Some of the reasons are the same in the two cases, but the manner is different. For Luke too the End, though of vital importance, is not immediate. More than in the case of Matthew, however, it has shed its qualitative difference from present, earthly existence, and has become something more like the last in the series of events in which mankind is already immersed: tomorrow, tomorrow, tomorrow, then the End; less the decisive act of God, more the end of the story. It could hardly be otherwise for Luke, for telling the story, narrating the course of events, is his essential idiom. He is the historian, who looks out on society to watch and report, not indeed dispassionately – he knows what the sequence means in the purposes of God and how great are the demands it makes upon men – but with a considerable degree of interest in events and their participants for their own sake (Acts xi, 28; xiii, 1; xviii, 12; Luke ii, 1; iii, 1). Here too he differs from Matthew. Whatever his supernatural origins, Jesus himself becomes in large measure 'a historical figure', described in the categories of narrative rather than the technical terms of theology. So for Luke it is impossible to present Jesus' passion and death as other than a poignant tragedy – as such a death would be to any sympathetic narrator – and the sadness can only be relieved when it is reversed by the succeeding events of resurrection and ascension. (Contrast John's presentation of the death as itself the moment of consummation and glory.) Only the barest minimum of conceptual language is to be discovered in Luke (he seems even deliberately to refuse it, cf. his omission of Mark x, 45); his whole manner discourages it. Luke's story of Jesus, then, has much of the cast of the tale of a hero. He is, of course, as in

Matthew, also the teacher, but this is not primary: he is above all the gracious bringer of salvation who lives and dies for the simple and the outcast, that they might turn to God (iv, 16ff.; xv, 1ff.; xix, 1–10).

For such a writer it is not surprising that ethics appear in terms of simple human virtue, above all in terms of social generosity – for which Christ in life and death was the supreme and heroic model. For him, by contrast with Matthew, the jewish Law is seen as simply abrogated or superseded whenever it conflicts with the demands of this simple ethic. Luke, unlike Matthew, feels no need to support his deviations by argument from the Law itself (compare Luke vi, 1–11 with Matthew xii, 1–14).

The inhumanity of the sabbath law meets the opposition of Jesus more frequently in Luke than elsewhere; xiii, 10–17 and xiv, 1–6 are stories found in Luke alone; vi, 1–5 and 6–11 are from Mark, but the Lukan teaching is made plain. Thus, in the story of the healing of the man with the withered hand (cf. p. 50), he retains from Mark the saying which says what is at stake ('is it lawful on the sabbath to do good or to do ill, to save life or to kill?') – which Matthew had dropped (vi, 9; cf. Mark iii, 4; Matt. xii, 11). But he omits Mark's statement that Jesus looked round at his critics 'with anger, being grieved at the hardness of their hearts,' thus modifying the sharpness of the confrontation between two whole worlds. While Mark's Jesus proclaims among sinful men the stark challenge of the Kingdom, Luke's Jesus is the examplar of generous and effective compassion for all in need. In this humane picture of Jesus, anger lacked the place which it appropriately possessed in the darker, 'theological' portrayal provided by Mark.

The same message appears in Luke's illustration of the command to love the neighbour by giving the story of the Good Samaritan: the command means for Luke generosity which goes beyond all expectation. Not only is the Law, which forbids the priest and the Levite to defile themselves by contact with what might turn out to be a corpse, dismissed out of hand for obstructing fundamental moral duty; but that duty is shown to extend to all in need, even to those whom the Law counts as beyond the pale – and a Samaritan (a member of a despised religious minority) can see it! For him, the injured *Jew* has no claim according to the Law. His act shows up the hollowness of rabbinic argument about the boundaries of the operation of the command to love the neighbour.

Along with the exhortation to generosity goes the commendation of poverty. Luke's beatitudes (vi, 20f.) show Jesus assuring his disciples of the blessedness of poverty and hunger in their literal sense (contrast Matt. v, 3, 6), and the teaching is emphasized by the addition of corresponding 'woes' (vi, 24f.). In the Acts of the Apostles, simple poverty, in the shape of community of property, is a hallmark of the original Jerusalem congregation in what Luke undoubtedly regarded as the Church's golden age (Acts ii, 44; iv, 32–7). It is no accident that the only occasion on which Luke's serene sunlit portrayal of the gospel's onward progress is darkened is in reporting the failure of Ananias and Sapphira to cast into the common fund the whole of the proceeds of the sale of their property (v, 1–11). Their sin may seem to us to be met by over-severe retribution, but this is the measure of the seriousness in Luke's eyes of disciples' refusal to accept Jesus' teaching and example in this matter (cf. Luke xvi, 14, and the story of Lazarus, xvi, 19–31). It is for Luke one of the crucial tests of allegiance, and it is likely that in his mind to take up the cross *daily* (ix, 23; contrast Mark viii, 34) is to adopt precisely this mode of persistent sacrificial conduct (cf. 'with endurance' in viii, 15) which expresses itself most practically in the bestowal of one's goods. It is not surprising that the one saying of Jesus which appears in Acts (xx, 35) – it occurs in Paul's key, farewell speech to the elders of the church of Ephesus, his only speech to a christian audience – is: 'It is more blessed to give than to receive.' Nor is it surprising that at the begining of the story, the preaching of John the Baptist, in Luke's version, includes the same ethical motifs as the teaching of Jesus (Luke iii, 10–14).

Because of the character of one's Lord generosity of heart in bestowing one's allegiance gives rise to generosity with one's property. Yet this remains a moral attitude, in the first sphere as in the second: it does not turn into a philosophy about 'the world'. Unlike John, Luke does not link contempt for property and costly giving of oneself to Christ (xiv, 26f.) with radical separateness from the world on grounds of fundamental theological principle. Rather, love is to be directed not merely to fellow-Christians but precisely to those who have no natural or legal claim – the man attacked by robbers (x, 29ff.), the thief on the cross (xxiii, 39ff.) and one's attackers (xxiii, 34). This is what taking up the cross daily (ix, 23) and *carrying* the cross (xiv, 27, contrast Matthew's *receive*, x, 38) mean: decision for Christ merges into faithful moral action along the lines he so powerfully laid down by example and precept.

We are very far here from the Fourth Gospel's command to 'love *one another*'. There love is the bond of the community – a whole mode of life, a quality of existence. In Luke, it is a virtue with clear and definite practical expression, a matter of cash, property and service, given by those who know that much has been done for them by their self-giving Lord. The anointing of Jesus by the woman (vii, 36ff.), removed from the context of the Passion where Mark sets it, is no longer a sign which foreshadows his burial (Mark xiv, 8) but the expression of a sinner's love (vii, 47), met by divine forgiveness.

However, generosity for Luke is not a human virtue, in the sense of an admirable quality which a man generates within himself and practises on his own impulse. It springs from the warm response of the heart to the gift received. Although his idiom is less theological and more practical, Luke is not at variance with the Pauline teaching that divine grace precedes and empowers man's moral action, the fruit of the Spirit (Gal. v, 22). His teaching is also paralleled in John (xv, 9–12; I John iv, 10), where the love of the brotherhood depends upon the love of the Father mediated through the Son, and in Matthew, where only acceptance into the company of Jesus makes operative the following of the commands which he has given (xxviii, 16–20).

Luke's variant on this theme is exemplified in numerous episodes: the story of Zacchaeus, who is impelled by acceptance by Jesus to give away his goods (xix, 1–10); the story of the lepers, where Jesus' gift evokes from one alone the generous response of gratitude (xvii, 11–19); the story of the rich ruler (xviii, 18–30, from Mark); the episode of the thief whose penitence is aroused by the mere presence of Jesus (xxiii, 39–43); the story of the two sons, where the father's love and the recognition of the son in his desperate need is the condition for the homecoming's being achieved (xv, 11–32); the parable of the supper, where those who refuse to accept the generosity offered to them can have no share in the meal (xiv, 12–24).

So two strands meet: the need for man to see both his need for God and the stringency of God's demand (and Luke can state that in sharper terms than the other evangelists, xiv, 25ff.), and God's graciousness as that which alone brings about a life in the path of virtue; where man in relation to those around him expresses, in appropriate manner, the same love which has been lavished upon him by God (vi, 27–38): 'Be merciful, even as your Father is merciful' (vi, 36).

(On the Acts of the Apostles, and Luke's attitude to the Law, see also next section.)

(vi) PAUL INTERPRETED

The ambiguity and subtlety of Paul's attitude to the Law (cf. pp. 32f.) was not maintained by his interpreters in the early Church. This need cause no surprise. On the one hand, Paul's teaching sprang straight from his own circumstances as a Pharisee (and one with a particular range of religious experience) converted to faith in Jesus (and a faith of a specific colour and certain sharply formed features). Those who came to read him and to regard him as an authority could not share the impulses which chiefly moved him. On the other hand, they themselves were moved by equally powerful but different forces, dictated by the conditions of their times.

The picture of Paul drawn in Acts already shows the beginnings of this process. Here Paul no longer shows any sign of being tortured in his soul by the ruinous effects on man of that Law which was nevertheless a divine providence; here there is no radical rejection of the Law as in effect wholly useless as the means to man's right relationship with God. Rather, the Law is partly acceptable, partly not – and the measure is not the question of man's standing *vis à vis* God, but expediency and pastoral possibilities. It is a matter of what can reasonably and suitably be demanded. The former consideration is to be seen in Acts xv and results in the minimal commands imposed on gentile converts in the decree agreed at the Council (xv, 20); the latter appears in incidents such as the taking of the Nazirite vow (xviii, 18; xxi, 23ff.) and the circumcision of Timothy (xvi, 1ff.), where Paul (by contrast with his own account of his policy in the case of Titus, Gal. ii, 3) accepts, in a borderline case, a requirement of the Law which is not to be demanded of pure Gentiles entering the Church (xv). Like the apostles in the earlier chapters of Acts, Paul is presented as making no total break with Judaism, but as continuing to associate himself with its rites and ceremonies, in particular with the Temple (for example, iii, 1; xxi, 27).

His acceptance of the decree at the Council (xv, 20) makes the same point. These commands are a mark of the continuity of the new Jew–Gentile Church, of which the Council is in Luke's eyes the inauguration ceremony, with the Israel of the old covenant. Their source lies probably in the conditions which, according to Deuteronomy xii, are to be observed when Israel has come to live in the land of promise, the time of fulfilment which foreshadows that now realized in the establishing of the Church and the launching of her mission to Jews and Gentiles alike. Deuteronomy commands an end to idolatry (xii, 1ff.), then common meals for all ('the unclean and the clean', i.e. Jews and non-Jews), except that 'you shall not eat the blood' (xii, 15f.), provisions precisely those of the Council's decree (provided *porneia*, in any case doubtfully original in the text, is taken to mean idolatry.) [12]

Whatever the historical truth in this picture, it represents the mind of Luke for whom the roots of Christianity in Judaism are essential – and in whose circle they were perhaps already being challenged, as later they were to be by Marcion. It is therefore a major element in his concern to make plain their importance.

For Luke, admittedly, it is not the legal and moral requirements of Judaism whose validity is to be defended but the religion itself as the providential background to Christ and

12. This suggestion is made in the unpublished Oxford doctoral thesis by J. L. Keedy, *St Luke's Account of the Travels of St Paul* (1970), pp. 8off.

the Church: Christianity is no novel mystery cult but rooted in the age-long purposes of God (cf. Luke i-ii; iii, 23–38). In answer to the question whether the Law retains validity for Christians, Matthew's Yes and Paul's Yes-and-No are matched by a Lukan Partly. By what criteria then did he distinguish between different elements in the Law? Not it appears by jettisoning the ceremonial and retaining the moral commands.[13] The elements of the Law which the Paul of Acts accepts are all ceremonial, whether it is circumcision in the case of Timothy (xvi, 1ff.), or the regulations for gentile converts (xv, 20), agreed by the Jerusalem Council, or the Nazirite vow taken by Paul.[14] But in Luke's eyes, none of these episodes is seen as concerned with devotion to the Law as such: all are signs that the Church is rooted in the history of God's saving work, that there has been no radical break, and that the Church, now consisting of both Jews and Gentiles, is the wholly legitimate heir of Israel, continuing the old while blossoming into new life under Jesus, the exalted Messiah. For making this clear, these institutions of Judaism are much more impressive symbols than the continuation of jewish moral rules alone.

It is interesting that, in line with Luke's attitude in the Gospel (cf. p. 56), the sabbath nowhere appears in Acts as one of the examples of approved continuity: it is mentioned simply as the day when gatherings of Jews can be encountered and preached to, Acts xiii, 14; xvi, 13; xvii, 2; xviii, 4. Sabbath observance is too closely bound to attitudes which are anathema to Luke – meanness of heart and hypocritical pride.

13. As, for example, Valentinian Gnostic Christians did in the second century, cf. Ptolomaeus' 'Letter to Flora,' ed. R. M. Grant, *Gnosticism* (London, 1961), pp. 184ff.

14. All ceremonial, with the possible exception of *porneia*, xv, 20: which may mean fornication in the common sense or refer to idolatry, seen, as in the Old Testament, as unfaithfulness to God.

We saw in the last section that as far as the moral law is concerned Luke's emphasis on generous compassion overshadows all else. He repeats Mark's story of the rich man (he calls him a ruler), which endorses the moral requirements of the Decalogue (xviii, 18ff.), and gives a strict form of the forbidding of divorce – like Matthew v, 32, but without the exception clause (xvi, 18). One problem remains: how does Luke xvi, 17 accord with the interpretation we have put forward of Luke's attitude to the Law, especially as it appears in Acts? If we are not to admit that Luke simply reports what he receives, regardless of making sense in relation to the context and to his whole outlook, it is hard to see how, in view of xvi, 16, this verse can have been intended in its plain sense. How can the Law be both obsolete since John the Baptist's appearance and valid in every detail until the world's end? In the light of the attack on the Pharisees in the previous verse, it must surely be ironical: though the Law, in the full sense, has now had its day (verse 16), heaven and earth might disappear for all the notice the Pharisees take of the fact, so distorted is their perception of God's ways (cf. xi, 39–52; xviii, 9–14). This view is confirmed by verse 18 which is different from and stricter than the Law's teaching on divorce. (On verse 18, see also p. 79.)

In the Pastoral Epistles, Paul's teaching about the Law finds another adaptation, once more one for which even restrained imagination does not find it difficult to find an explanation in the circumstances of the Church of the late first or early second century. Here Paul's Yes-and-No to the Law is replaced not by a partly-Yes-and-partly-No, but by a firm Yes – only now it is not to the Jewish Law but to moral law in itself. Morality and orthodoxy are the twin pillars of this writer's outlook (I Tim. i, 3–5, 19; iii, 9f.; iv, 7–12, 15f.; vi, 11, 20; II Tim. i, 14; ii, 14–16; iv, 3; Titus ii, 1); and from the facts that he is rarely specific about the contents of the latter and impatient about doctrinal controversy (Titus iii, 9), while he readily gives lists of vices to be shunned and virtues to be embraced, it looks as if he sees christian life most clearly in moral terms (Titus iii, 8). For him there is no doubt that 'the Law [i.e. morality in general] is good' (I Tim. i, 8). What is most notable is that there are only the haziest lines of reasoning joining his faith to his morality. He speaks of the two in harness with each other (e.g. I Tim. i, 19), but the logic by which the one gives rise to the other or authorizes it is never stated. Rather, the goodness of moral qualities is simply assumed: they are common ground between him and his readers. Moreover, the virtues and vices listed are the commonplaces of moral systems, owing more to the ethics of the contemporary world than any specifically christian inspiration (e.g. Titus ii, 2ff.). Temperance, good sense and piety are his favourite qualities; profligacy and foolishness of talk and behaviour the sins most hated (Titus i, 10; II Tim. ii, 16).[15]

We are close here to an autonomous ethic (cf. pp. 6f.). Though the Judgement is still in view (II Tim. iv, 8), it appears in a passage in which the writer movingly adopts the persona of Paul who looks forward serenely to that day; and though the great acts of Christ and the grace that flows from them are recalled (e.g. II Tim. i, 9f.; ii, 8), they nowhere directly affect the contents or the proportions of the moral teaching. Neither an urgent eschatology nor a live sense of existence centred on Christ seem to exert any pressure upon the ethics.

This leads to negative and positive inferences about the situation in which these epistles were written. Negatively, the End was surely no longer regarded as imminent, and the

15. See C. K. Barrett, *The Pastoral Epistles* (Oxford, 1963), pp. 25–8.

christian proclamation had begun to settle into a system of orthodox teaching needing to be safeguarded. It had somewhat lost its sharp cutting-edge, that capacity to inform every aspect of thought and life which is so evident in Paul. Positively, the Church of this writer felt the need for defence and retrenchment: positions must be made secure against divisive, mistaken and wicked forces (e.g. I Tim. i, 20), which were threatening the security of those who felt themselves to be the authentic representatives of the central tradition and the heirs of Paul. For this purpose it was essential to present Paul as the unambiguous supporter of moral law. The thought of the historical Paul was, even in his lifetime, easily interpreted as antinomian (Rom. iii, 31). Not a hint of that charge must be allowed to stick and the writer of the Pastoral Epistles make it impossible.

The story could be taken further. After the period witnessed to in the New Testament, christian writers continued to soften and modify the sharp lines of Paul's teaching on the Law, usually to oppose groups antinomian by principle, or else in the constant struggle to keep up moral standards. In general, they carried further the process which the Pastoral Epistles and, in its different way (from a concern more to do with the unity of God's purposes in history than with ethics), the Acts of the Apostles had begun, of smoothing over every hint of depreciation of law.[16] The development reaches its terminus in the christian art of the fifth century, where Christ is portrayed giving to Paul the scroll of his law for him to promulgate as his apostle.[17]

16. M. F. Wiles, *The Divine Apostle* (Cambridge, 1967), chapter IV.

17. W. F. Volbach, *Early Christian Art* (London, 1961), plates 174 and 178, and pp. 345f.

(vii) JAMES

The ethics of the Epistle of James are, from the point of view of conceptual pattern, the simplest in the New Testament: no theological impulse overtly provides them with backing and the writer embraces a simple belief in practical charity, humble endurance and control of the tongue as the keys to moral life. Yet he is not without a vision, for this is a 'law of liberty', centring on love of one's neighbour (i, 25; ii, 8, 12), which man will be enabled to keep through the word of God (i, 21). So even in this theologically undeveloped work the priority of God's action is maintained securely.

(viii) CONCLUSIONS

Our survey of the ethical teaching of a selection of leading New Testament writers enables us to look at the doctrinal forces at work in the early Church (set out in chapter 1) in a different perspective. In the light of that opening analysis, it now seems that the ethical standpoint of a New Testament writer is related to two chief variables.

First, eschatology. The further away a writer thinks the End to be or the less (in a particular context) he has his eyes upon it, the more autonomous his ethics. If the End is removed from immediate view, then ethics come into their own as the object of independent interest. Moreover, though the content of the teaching may still be subject to other powerful doctrinal pressures (as, in Matthew, the continuing validity of God's Law given to Israel, or, in Luke, the character of Jesus as the writer sees him), it tends to be inspired by the needs of harmonious and stable social life, centred in the Church, and to be directed towards its maintenance. This, as we have seen, is the case with Matthew (though the ultimate Judgement is never far from his sight), Luke–Acts,

James and the Pastoral Epistles. In all these works, a high value is set on moral principles which, with whatever modifications, would for the most part be acceptable in any civilized society. The Pastoral Epistles and the Epistle of James in particular show, in their ethics, hardly any features which depend directly on christian faith.

The point is immediately clear if the teaching of these works is contrasted with the moral values implicit in a writing which we have not discussed, the Apocalypse of John. There, in the unique crisis of the world's history, customary morals will be suspended. Slaughter and bloodshed on a vast scale, warfare and hostility – these are now expected features of human behaviour. No longer reprehensible, indeed regarded as outside the sphere of moral judgement altogether, they are part and parcel of the emergency which will ineluctably arise in a state of wholesale abnormality. In the state of affairs depicted here, moral concern disappears from sight: the drama of God must work itself out.

In Paul and Mark, we found signs of the same cast of thought, but in Paul it does not represent the whole of his mind. Sometimes he writes, in response to practical needs, as if the End were far away.

But a writer's ethical standpoint may not be read off, as it were, by taking his eschatological temperature. A second test must be applied: that of the value given to 'the world', whether by that is meant simply society apart from the Church or, on the basis of a more elaborate philosophical outlook, the universe as a material, transient entity contrasted with the divine sphere which alone has enduring significance. In effect, the less valuable the world is reckoned to be, the less autonomy and prominence ethics receive. For Luke, for example, the world is of genuine interest and constitutes the sphere within which the Church conducts its mission and towards which it has to define its attitude and stance. Ethics are for him a constant preoccupation, and, however much his scale of values depends upon his picture of Jesus, the moral attitudes which he recommends are intelligible in their own right. In the Gospel of John, by contrast, where 'the world' is certainly not, in the end, the object of optimistic hope, ethics are on the way to being subsumed under theology. The writer is so concerned to establish and identify the environment of belief in which the christian community exists over against the world that he has no interest in the intricacies of practical moral problems. It suffices if the brothers love one another. The one essential thing is to have that mark of the common life assured.

In comparing these two gospels, we can see the need to apply both our tests, for though neither writer believes the End to be on the threshold, they differ radically in their manner of reacting to the loss of that belief. Luke turns to the world and tries to see how the Church relates to it and finds a place in its life and history. John turns from the world and within the enclosed area of the Church finds the chief features of the coming age (like eternal life and the Spirit's presence) already anticipated. His 'low' evaluation of the world is the condition for his realized eschatology. (Perhaps we should reverse this: his realized eschatology is the condition for his evaluation. It depends on whether the writer is seen as a Christian whose mentality is not inaccurately described as gnostic (see p. 35) in tendency. It is sometimes held that his realized eschatology is a survival and development of very early christian belief in the immediacy of the End, which was regarded as already breaking in with the preaching of Jesus and above all his resurrection. The difficulty is that John has gone so far in applying the language of the future age to the Church's present and in abandoning any live sense of the End's future appearance (apart from mention of it in v, 28f.; vi, 40, 54; xii, 48) that this view hardly commends itself. Besides, there are so many other signs that, however primitive the roots of some of its material, the conceptional affinities of this work are to be sought elsewhere than in the earliest palestinian Christianity.)

The book that is perhaps most illuminated by the application of our calculus is the Gospel of Mark – always an enigma when it comes to locating the writer's mind on the thought-map of the early Church. Ethics for him are neither prominent nor significant for their own sake; and they certainly do not approach autonomous status. Can we then 'read off' the evangelist's theological standpoint? Is his treatment of ethics to be attributed to a belief that the End is near or to a depreciation of the world, a tendency to an esoteric concept of christian faith and life? Or is it to be laid at the door of a third doctrinal pressure – a strong sense of the authoritative status and will of Jesus? In our account of the Gospel of Mark, we saw reason to believe that all three forces are at work. There is much to be said for the view that he wrote in the context of a revival of eschatological 'fever', perhaps in the Jewish War of A.D. 66–70; there is much evidence that for him the possession of the mystery of the Gospel was a prize to be attained only with difficulty; and undoubtedly Jesus was in all things decisive – why else did he, first of all Christians, take up the task of writing 'the gospel of Jesus Christ' (i, 1)? And if it is alleged, against the view that for him the End was near, that no man would have written down the story of Jesus at such a juncture, may not his sense of the centrality of Jesus, now as living and authoritative as ever, be sufficient answer?[18]

18. See É Trocmé, *La Formation de l'Évangile selon Marc* (Paris, 1963).

3. The Problems

WE now turn to another approach to the New Testament literature as evidence for the ethical thought of the early Church, and here, as in our survey of the leading writers, we shall find ourselves confronted with diversity.

Like the christian community of all periods, the Church of the first two or three generations had moral problems which pressed for solution. Christians were faced with dilemmas and difficulties, and compelled to work for answers to them. What tools were available to them? How did they use them, and what conclusions did they reach? These are the questions with which this chapter deals. We shall limit ourselves to the consideration of a small number of important problems, all of which remain alive in one form or another. Here we see the beginnings of some of the traditional solutions. Other New Testament answers failed to survive. However great the authority soon accorded to the New Testament as canonized scripture, they had become impossible to apply in changed circumstances or simply no longer carried conviction. We make no attempt at a full exegesis of the passages referred to: that work has been done elsewhere time and again. Our discussion aims to be sufficient to show the lines of reasoning which led to the various solutions and to make plain why that diversity, which has continued and become ever more complex, was inevitable from the Church's earliest years.

The variety was inevitable, if for no other reason, because ethics were not the Church's primary concern. Not ethics but allegiance to God's work in and through Christ gave the Church its cohesion. Moreover, variety appeared not only in the moral thinking but already in the doctrinal expression of that allegiance – and doctrine both was more fundamental than ethics and, as we have seen, tended to determine their shape. The Church's patterns of ethical thought and its practical decisions were derivative – and were not always the outcome of the most stringent christian reflection.

In these circumstances, the early Church, it seems, did not find itself equipped with an ethic, but rather engaged in a quest for ethical principles, which in the period covered by the New Testament did not result in many agreed solutions. This is the only conclusion we can draw from the variety of teaching to be found in the New Testament, once we get away from the most general principles; and even then, their context and the relative weight given to this principle rather than that differ for reasons related to the writer's outlook and circumstances. In the gospels, particularly those of Matthew and Luke, Jesus appears, of course, as the giver of clear and often detailed moral teaching; but not only are their presentations of his teaching not in agreement, whether in content or in emphasis, but the rest of the New Testament shows how little an authoritative and clear tradition of that teaching survived and was available. The teaching Jesus of these gospels is scarcely recognizable in the moral ideals of the Pastoral Epistles and James. Even as early as Paul, despite a reference to Jesus' teaching on divorce (I Cor. vii, 10) and a number of similarities to his teaching as presented in the gospels,[1] it can hardly be claimed that recognition and knowledge of that teaching as Jesus' own is as clear as the day. In any case, even if there had been a clear perception of a need to preserve his teaching intact and of the manifold risks of its being shifted and modified, new circumstances

1. A. M. Hunter makes the most of their significance in *Paul and his Predecessors* (London, 1940).

and new demands would inevitably have altered it, in nuance if not in principle.

Even the priority of the command to love is, despite initial appearances, no exception. Here we seem to have a key principle, a touchstone, by which moral action and all other commands were to be judged. But though this command appears in all the major writers (Paul and the evangelists, as well as James and I Peter), the form and bearing are different in each case. In Paul it is seen as the summary of the second half of the Decalogue and 'of any other commandment' (Rom. xiii, 9f.; Gal. v, 14). In Mark (xii, 31ff.) it is the greatest command in the Law and superior to the offering of sacrifices. In Matthew, on the contrary, it is that on which the whole Law depends (xxii, 39f.), so that even the ritual system is presumably to be regarded as expressing the command to love God and one's neighbour. In Luke, the rest of the teaching makes it likely that the command to love one's neighbour is understood in the most straightforward terms of sacrificial generosity (x, 29ff.). In Matthew and Luke, there is in addition the wider command to love enemies (Matt. v, 44; Luke vi, 27), and indeed in the latter gospel, the story of the Good Samaritan interprets the command to love one's neighbour in something approaching this sense. In John (xiii, 34), on the other hand, the ethical horizon is narrowed and intensified to the love of the fellow-Christian, love within the community, in the setting of a profound and highly integrated theological perspective. For Paul, the universality of the scope of the command to love seems to be implicit in I Corinthians xiii, though there is no explicit mention there of those towards whom it is to be exercised.

Moreover, the absence of this priority from other writings is perhaps as significant, from the point of view of obtaining a just picture of the ethical teaching of the early Church, as its centrality in these five writers (cf. also I Peter iv, 8 –

'above all . . . love one another'; and James ii, 8, where, as in Matthew, obedience to the command to love the neighbour entails obedience to the whole Law). In the Pastoral Epistles, love is placed alongside other qualities (I Tim. i, 14; ii, 15; iv, 12; vi, 11; II Tim. i, 7, 13; ii, 22; iii, 10; Titus ii, 2), and has lost the brilliance with which it stands out in the books we have just discussed. The verb *to love* does not appear once. In the admittedly limited ethical matter in the Epistle to the Hebrews, the verb does not occur and x, 24 gives the only reference to love as a desirable christian quality.

As far as this negative evidence goes, it appears that not all early christian circles were as single-mindedly dedicated to a 'love morality' (whatever precisely that may mean) as is often supposed, and that even those which might be thus described meant by it many different things, ranging from the intra-community love of the Fourth Gospel to the devotion to the Torah in Matthew.

(i) DIVORCE

Does the New Testament (or does Jesus) teach unambiguously the indissolubility of marriage? It is still often held, as if there were no doubt about the matter, that the answer is a clear Yes – and a Yes that can brook no further questions, raise no possibility of light and shade. What does the New Testament say?[2] Or, to rephrase the question, what range of opinion and practice existed in the Church of the first century?

Against the background of Roman society, in which divorce was easy for both husband and wife, and Judaism, in which it was generally more difficult than in Roman law,

2. See *Marriage, Divorce and the Church* (report of a commission appointed by the Archbishop of Canterbury, London, 1971), Appendix A by Hugh Montefiore and Appendix B by John Bowker.

but nevertheless possible[3] (sometimes mandatory) for the husband, the New Testament is held to give clear, strict and almost unanimous teaching. The exceptions are Matthew, who allows divorce in one specified class of case (v, 32; xix, 9), and Paul, who countenances it in mixed marriages (I Cor. vii, 15).

In fact, 'the New Testament' in this case means four witnesses – Paul and the first three gospels. No other New Testament writer offers any evidence, and as many of them contain much ethical material, this may indicate that the problem was not of central importance within the christian body. Once the congregations began to be established, possibly their cohesion and distinctness from society at large made the question less likely to arise within the christian ranks, and it was largely to the needs of their own community that these writers confined their attention.

However, there are our four witnesses. Is it fair to see them as virtually unanimous?

Paul. His teaching is to be found in I Corinthians vii, 10–15. Verses 10 and 11 are addressed to christian couples; verses 12–15 to those who have a pagan partner ('to the rest'). Three principles are to be noted. First, marriage creates a perfectly objective 'solidarity' (cf. union with a prostitute where the same is true, vi, 16). Divorce is therefore in principle impossible, and if separation occurs no remarriage can take place, so that the way may be open for the reunion of the estranged couple. Nevertheless, 'God has called us to peace' (verse 15), and in cases of mixed marriage this second principle may triumph over the first. The christian partner is at liberty to separate if the pagan partner wishes it, though perhaps the first principle still holds sway in such cases to the degree that remarriage is not to occur – Paul does not

3. The conditions were in dispute. See Montefiore, op. cit., pp. 79f.

specifically state this, but it is likely. His emphasis seems to be that in mixed marriages such separation, though permissible, is by no means mandatory. The teaching here is possibly to be seen in the light of vi, 12ff.: becoming a Christian creates a new solidarity (becoming 'united to the Lord', vi, 17 – using a term for sexual union), which may supersede the existing marriage to a pagan. (Cf. p. 26.)

The third principle is the ruling from the Lord which authorizes the forbidding of divorce (verse 10). Paul takes this as applying strictly only to marriages where both parties are Christians. It is not then, in his view, a command concerning marriage as such, but only certain marriages.

The position is then that Paul is not legislating for all marriages (the question of divorce in general is never raised), but only for those involving Christians; and in one class of such marriages, those where one partner is pagan, the marriage is dissoluble at will, and the Lord's veto is taken to refer only to fully christian marriages. Why is separation on the ground of religious difference allowed? The answer is clear: the End is close, and in the forefront of Paul's mind is the question: who is to be in the company of the saved? Plainly, those who believe in the Lord. But what of those who do not believe, but are joined to believers by the marriage-bond? So strong and real is the bond for Paul the Jew that such persons will clearly share in the salvation of their christian partners – unless they positively opt out by separation; and this they may prefer to do. It may not make for peace for them to stay where, bluntly, they will not be in place (verses 14 and 15). 'Consecration' (verse 14), that is membership of the holy community of God's people, and 'salvation' (verse 16), that is acceptance on the Last Day, are open to them, but may be declined. Here, as in the rest of chapter vii, Paul's eye is on the imminent End.

It is possible that this account of Paul's teaching is

seriously out of focus. On the basis of rabbinic doctrine, Dr David Daube has suggested that Paul's view is in effect quite the opposite of what it seems to the modern reader.[4] The rabbis taught (and teach) that conversion to Judaism means the end of all existing relationships: a convert is as a new-born babe. Paul reflects this in relation to christian converts in II Corinthians v, 17: 'If any one is in Christ, he is a new creation.' The rabbis taught further that a convert was therefore free to marry even those to whom marriage would formerly have been forbidden (e.g. as incestuous), unless such a marriage would give scandal because it was contrary to the customs of surrounding gentile society. If this teaching is the model for Paul, then the liberty of the pagan partner to leave a christian husband or wife is no concession (so much for the 'Pauline privilege' of traditional terminology), but rather the natural expression of the convert's 'new-born' state. In terms of doctrine, it is exceptional that the partner should remain. He (or she) may, however, do so, according to Daube, for the sake of peace (verse 15; cf. Paul's solicitude for the weaker brethren in the matter of eating meat that had been consecrated at pagan temples, I Corinthians viii), or in the hope of converting the pagan partner (verse 16). But how *can* their marriage be continued if conversion ends all relationships? The answer (again, on rabbinic parallel) is: by their continued cohabitation. This itself constitutes a fresh marriage and it is in this sense that the unbelieving partner is 'consecrated' – a jewish groom says to his bride, 'Behold thou art consecrated unto me,' that is, our marriage is hereby contracted. Manifestly, as the Church has not retained the jewish concept of the radical effect of conversion,

4. 'Pauline Contributions to a Pluralistic Culture', in D. G. Miller and D. Y. Hadidian (eds.) *Jesus and Man's Hope*, II (Pittsburgh, 1971), pp. 223ff.

it is hard to find a direct application for Paul's teaching on divorce in this kind of case.

Apart from the fact that Paul sees the argument for 'peace' (verse 15) applying not to the retaining but to the setting free of the pagan partner, the major difficulty with this interpretation of Paul is that the passage never states and does not seem to assume that conversion has brought any existing marriage to an automatic end, so that positive action (be it only continued cohabitation) is required for its continuance. Rather, he writes in terms of divorce being the positive step that may be taken (verses 12 and 13).

Mark (x, 1–12). Divorce is forbidden, *tout court*, with the authority of the Lord's word. So far Paul is confirmed. But the argument and the setting are quite different. Here, the imminence of the End plays no explicit part. There is no casuistry concerning mixed christian and pagan marriages or concerning hard cases of any sort. Must we then accuse Mark (and if he reports *ipsissima verba*, Jesus himself) of a lack of realism, a failure to provide for inevitable practical problems? To read the passage thus is to misread it. This is not a contribution to a debate about grounds for divorce, it is chiefly a theological statement about marriage. Behind the deuteronomic concession to human weakness stands Genesis i, 27 – God's original gracious purpose for man, now, in the coming of Jesus, at length to be fulfilled. Paradise is to be re-established.

It is not clear whether Mark sees this as teaching which is valid for all men: the passage is addressed to Pharisees in the presence of the crowds. We should probably see it as cast at them in the way of challenge. Once more, as constantly in Mark, Jesus proclaims the kingdom of God and its ways in the face of those who will not hear. But in the circle of his people, Mark's readers, his path will be followed. This, then, is teaching concerning marriage *as such*, but nothing short of acceptance of God's kingdom will make it possible for man to keep it. Such, in the context of Mark's Gospel as a whole, seems to be the sense of the passage.

Matthew (xix, 3–12; v, 32). In comparison with Mark, Matthew removes the possibility that the wife should ever be the initiator of divorce – his background is that of jewish, not Roman, customs (cf. Mark x, 11) – and, more important, turns the passage into a discussion about the grounds for divorce (xix, 3 'for any cause'). This transforms its sense. Having raised the legal·question, Matthew provides an answer: divorce is to be allowed on grounds of *porneia*, probably to be taken in the general sense of sexual misconduct. He is then legislating for the (at least, his) christian community in line with the stricter of the two current jewish schools, that of Rabbi Shammai, whose view was finally to be defeated by that of Rabbi Hillel, who took the 'unclean thing' of Deuteronomy xxiv, 1 to mean whatever occasioned the displeasure of husbands. In line with his general pastoral and ethical concerns, the evangelist provides guidance for his congregation on a live controversy of the day, taking as usual a stringent view (cf. v, 22, 28, 34, 39, 44, 48).

Matthew is helped in changing the passage from a piece of doctrine to a piece of moral legislation by his switching of the order of the Genesis provision and Moses' concession. The former then appears as the basic law, which is modified or glossed, first by Moses' rule and now by the greater law of Jesus.

Of course, Matthew's ruling is not without a theological context. But here, as distinct from Mark, that context is the teaching, willing God, who requires obedience from his own and gives them sufficient commands. These commands are always, as we have seen, strenuous: it is surprising that this writer countenances divorce on any ground at all. It is a measure of both his jewishness (despite Mark's passage before his eyes) and the normality of divorce among Jews that he allows it, even though he goes with the stricter party. His ideals are high, as we see from the following passage (xix, 11f.) where celibacy is envisaged 'for the sake of the kingdom of heaven'. Among Jews none but the Essenes advocated that piece of asceticism for any of their members.

Luke (xvi, 18). This writer omits the long passage found in Mark and Matthew, and in a single sentence reproduces the gist of the Markan teaching; but he does it by taking Matthew v, 32 as a basis (apart from the exception clause) and joining to it (with necessary changes of syntax) a phrase from Mark x, 11, 'and marries another, commits adultery'. The Lukan treatment of the matter is then hardly emphatic, and it is perhaps worth noting that in the Acts of the Apostles no incident occurs in which the question is raised: Luke did not see it as a matter of central importance in the life of the Church as he knew it.

Indeed it may be that the dismissal of a wife is for him simply an instance of his cardinal sin of meanness, in the shape of callous cruelty. His reference to it is placed just before the story of the rich man and Lazarus, where this vice appears in deepest hue and is thoroughly castigated.

If this reading of the saying in its context is correct (it is easier for 18a than 18b, though possible for both), it may enable us to explain why Luke was content with this brief reference to the subject. He omitted Mark x, 1–12 because he was not interested in providing a comprehensive moral guide (like Matthew), and is not particularly at home with episodes imbued with profound but allusive theology (like

Mark). He may have read the Markan passage as ethics, felt that to devote so much space to this issue outran its importance to him, and decided that it was more telling to use the Lord's teaching on divorce as one more opportunity to give his central ethical message.

There is a vital common conviction about the relations between the sexes underlying the positions we have outlined. It meant an enhanced position for women which went quite beyond much jewish practice. But by the time our writers were at work, there had come from it four quite distinct lines, or at any rate contexts, or argument. Paul is situational and eschatological. His question is: what, in the light of the Lord's word and the imminence of the End, shall Christians do? Mark is concerned with theology: God's fundamental will in the matter and the nature of man. Matthew presents a rabbinic argument on the basis of the Torah: his concern is chiefly practical. Luke wishes to encourage compassion. Assuming that there was a word from Jesus which in some terms or other opposed divorce, we cannot tell what its context was, and already by the end of the first century, Christians had contextualized it in writing in four quite distinct ways. In practical terms, four distinct policies were available. How rough and ready then seems the tradition by which we live: which is to enforce upon Christians the Markan teaching in a Matthean spirit!

(ii) POLITICAL OBEDIENCE

It is generally held that the New Testament recommends unqualified subservience to the state, and any modifications which Christian political theorists have in the course of the centuries made to such a simple doctrine have been based on the introduction of other moral criteria, by way of counterweight, rather than on the teaching of the New Testament itself. But is the New Testament's teaching as monochrome as this?

Paul (Romans xiii, 1–7). This passage, read as so many words, is the charter for the unfettered operation of all political power. Put it into the context in which Paul lived, and the message becomes, if not necessarily different, at least wholly understandable. Certainly Paul cannot on any showing be credited with practical social or political radicalism; for example he was less critical than some thinkers of his time on the subject of slavery.[5] But naked authoritarianism is not a fair charge to level against him without careful qualification.

Two aspects of the context in which Paul wrote bear upon his judgement. First, the small size of the Church. Second, the imminence of the End, when Paul saw the Christians as destined, despite their small numbers, to judge mankind like the saints of the Most High in Daniel vii (I Cor. vi, 1f.) The policy urged in Romans xiii is then at most short-term. For the short time involved, Christians are to bear with the authorities under whom God has placed them. Moreover, the fact that God himself has so placed them is itself significant: it is not the subordinate powers of the universe (which have now been subjugated by Christ, cf. Colossians ii, 15), but God who makes this provision of government for mankind and gives an era of peace and stability. Paul is not in a position to be much alive to the great political world, which contained ample material for more critical estimates. He is content with the benefits of life in the Roman Empire as he knew it, for shortly the tribulations and distresses will come which are the inevitable prelude to the End (Rom. ii, 9; I Thess. v, 2ff.).

5. J. L. Houlden, *Paul's Letters from Prison* (Penguin, 1970), pp. 210ff.

Mark (xii, 13–17; cf. Matthew xxii, 15–22; Luke xx, 20–26). This passage came into discussion in the course of our outline of Mark's standpoint (p. 44), and we suggested that, in the context of Mark's teaching as a whole, it was not intended as a Markan statement of the teaching we have just seen in Paul. Its point was not, 'The state as well as God has its legitimate claims,' but 'The claims of God upon man are absolute, and man must face them; compared with them all other claims are trivial.' If this is what Mark meant, it does not of course exclude the possibility that, if used in the Church as an independent piece of tradition, before it came to be written into a book, it carried something much closer to the Pauline message and represented Jesus' authorization of it.

From another point of view, in the narrower Markan context, this is one of a series of episodes which show the storm-clouds gathering for the final crisis. In wave after wave, opponents endeavour to trap Jesus (xii, 13ff.), and soon his arrest and condemnation follow. From this angle, the story shows Jesus both vindicating himself and at the same time facing his attackers with the demand and judgement of God.

Whether in its probable sense when used independently or in what we have suggested is Mark's sense, the pressure of the End is not apparent in this story, as it is in Paul (Rom. xiii, 11). And in the latter sense, no practical political question is raised at all. This is simply one way of preaching the sovereignty of God, and as Mark presents it, it carries no explicit implications for a Christian's practical attitude to the state. The only place where this comes at all into view is in xiii, 9, where there is that uncritical, accepting and probably bewildered attitude to 'the powers that be' which is characteristic of the slum-dweller visiting the town hall. The little christian congregation is in no position to be formulating policy or 'having views' about anything as awesome, remote and powerful as the imperial government.

Luke however is more self-assured. He takes officials and administrators in his social stride and can, to a degree, look them in the eye. He is out to show, in this regard, that the Church, as an element in a complex society, is harmless and to be tolerated. He does this by showing that in its first years no government official (whether imperial or municipal, or even locally aristocratic like the Herods) ever thought it necessary to put a stop to christian activities, once he understood them: only when he was deceived or suborned by Jews did he ever adopt such a policy. It is true of Pilate himself (xxiii, 14f., 20, 22), as of Herod too; of Sergius Paulus (Acts xiii, 7–12), of the magistrates of Philippi (xvi, 35–9) and of Thessalonica (xvii, 8f.), of Gallio at Corinth (xviii, 12–17) and the town clerk at Ephesus (xix, 35–41), as well as of Paul's guards and interrogators (Claudias Lysias, Felix, Festus, and Herod Agrippa (xxiii–xxvi)). Luke even completes the picture by omitting the gruesome story of the execution of John the Baptist, and in referring to it in passing, leaves the impression that Herod's dominant impulse was a polite and cultured interest in Jesus and his movement (Luke ix, 9; cf. xxiii, 8; Acts xxvi).

There are two sides to Luke's teaching in this matter. On the one hand, it is an important piece of apologetic: Roman and other officials, concerned with law and order, have no need to oppress the christian body, for it is harmless, and no political charge levelled against it or its founder has ever had any basis (Luke xxiii 2; Acts xvii, 6). Whenever its leaders seem to have caused trouble, the blame should be laid at the door of quarrelsome and malicious Jews. In reality, the authorities would do well to think of the Church as one among the many parties in Judaism (Acts xxiv, 5, 14) – and so as worthy to enjoy the toleration accorded to the Jews and their religion.[6]

On the other hand, it is a piece of map-making for the Christians themselves. On these terms, they are to be ready to look the big imperial world squarely in the face and claim a place within it. The slum-dweller now lives in the suburbs and is no longer overawed by the municipal officials! Christians are to live in the Empire with as much assurance as others and to look for favourable treatment. In other words, Luke accepts political society as beneficent and stable, and life within it raises no moral issues whatsoever. Luke's polemic against meanness and cruelty never leads him to raise a voice against anyone in a position of political power, and in Luke xii, 14 perhaps Jesus is shown as one prepared to leave matters of civil justice to those whose task it is ('Man, who made me a judge or divider over you?'). Nowhere does he (or for that matter any other New Testament writer)extend this assured gaze of his so far as to lay down duties for those in authority. Being a good subject and citizen is the limit of his horizon in this respect. For him, it is likely that the story of the tribute money (xx, 20–26) does indeed signify the Lord's command that his followers must pay their taxes and his reassurance to sceptical outsiders that civil disobedience is not a game that Christians play.

In the latter part of the first century, the desire of the Church to settle down acceptably to a quiet existence in civil society, offering neither practical challenge nor even a theoretical critique, became strong. The Lukan atmosphere is reproduced in the firm adoption of 'establishment' attitudes in I Timothy ii, 2f. and I Peter ii, 13–15. The latter passage expresses complete confidence in the processes of imperial justice. The former seems to regard respectful loyalty on the

6. See H. J. Cadbury, *The Making of Luke-Acts* (London, 1958), ch. XX; B. S. Easton, *Early Christianity* (London, 1955), part two.

part of Christians as somehow the means to universal salvation – presumably because it will lead to the Church's being allowed to go about its mission quietly and thoroughly respectably. Already by the time I Timothy was written and probably by the date of I Peter, Christians had suffered some persecution at the hands of Roman authorities (at least that under Nero in Rome in A.D. 64); but this has done nothing to upset the confidence of these writers in the stable benevolence of the authorities.

This desire to merge quietly into the background did not always meet its just reward. When the Younger Pliny became the imperial governor in the disturbed province of Bithynia (the north-western corner of Asia Minor) in A.D. 111, he was sensitive to possible centres of sedition, and the groups which particularly attracted his attention were the Christians and the fire-brigade! In a letter to the Emperor Trajan he admits the harmlessness of christian morals and customs, but this is not enough to protect them.[7] The exclusiveness of their faith (cf. I Tim, ii, 5), showing itself in their refusal to take part in the cult of the emperor (akin to singing the national anthem on formal occasions), made them the objects of suspicion, as did the scandalous stories that were told about them. And reports of their practices aroused a quasi-aesthetic horror in a refined Roman like Pliny. It took this refusal to share in the ceremonies which upheld the social fabric to shake the wide religious tolerance of the Roman Empire (cf. p. 21). Only Jews (from time to time) and Druids aroused similar feelings – the former for their exclusiveness, the latter for being a focus of nationalist agitation.

In contrast to the Lukan line, *John* sees the imperial power

7. Letter X, 96, in *The Letters of the Younger Pliny* (Penguin, 1963), p. 293.

as a central expression of 'the world', which rejected Jesus and whose prince is the devil (xii, 31; xvi, 11). It is therefore not political power as such that John confronts, but the world, of which it is one aspect. But it is the aspect which, in the story of Jesus, takes the centre of the stage at the climax of the drama. In Pilate the world, represented by Roman authority, faces Jesus, and, with the blindness of the outsider whose justice is insufficient to the situation, condemns him.

In John's presentation, the confrontation is between two kings and two kingships (in Greek, *basileus* means both king and emperor), that which is 'of the world' and that which is not, the transient and the eternal. The drama is worked out in the long trial and its sequel in xviii, 33–xix, 22. Pilate's attempts to release Jesus here are on the surface similar to those in Luke – but the aim is now not to show that Jesus (and implicitly Christianity) is innocent of all harm, but to show that despite its attempt at justice (genuine at a certain level), the world's kingship is incapable of perceiving the truth (xviii, 37f.) and of resisting corruption of the heart (xix, 12–15). Therefore it becomes the devil's servant and the crucifier of the Son of God. Only those who come to the light, which is Jesus, can truly 'see' (ix, 39–41).

As always in John, the concern is much more theological than ethical. There is no counsel here about the degree of obedience a Christian should give to the state: John's Christians might well be living in a desert for all the aid they receive with this as indeed with other moral issues. Perhaps they were too insignificant ever to face such questions; perhaps John believed that, if theology is 'right', the rest can take care of itself.

The *Revelation to John* is in this respect close to the Fourth Gospel – but the song is set in a different key. Again there is the absolute confrontation, and the ranging of political power no longer among the friends of the Church but squarely with the enemies of God; again there is the assured divine victory, again the defeat of the forces of the world, but now the ultimate conflict is conducted with ferocious severity. The Empire is now no beneficent guarantor of peace but, as in the Gospel of John, the veritable incarnation of idolatrous power (Rev. xviii, 2, 10) – as indeed empires had been from the first days of apocalyptic writing in the Book of Daniel.

In this book, political imagery is carried one stage further by means of the time-honoured symbol of Jerusalem (cf. Isaiah lii, 1); the New Age, the consummation of God's purposes, is portrayed as a city, a 'new Jerusalem' (xxi, 2). The new life to be given by God to his own will be a civic life, wholly filled with his presence. How far any of the presentation is determined by a live hatred of the Roman Empire as a persecuting force, and how far it is part of the conventional scenario of apocalyptic speculation, it is hard to be sure.

What emerges from this range of attitudes as far as the question of political obedience is concerned? In each case, facets of the Church's life or thought in the early years are determinative for the attitudes displayed; whether it is desire for a stable existence (as in Acts and I Timothy), or a concern for dutiful obedience in the short period before the End (as in Romans), or perhaps the experience of trial and persecution in John's Apocalypse. The more profound theological doctrine of the Gospels of Mark and of John is of less direct ethical interest, but digs deep foundations for christian political theory in the future and poses a fundamental caveat to any unquestioning acceptance of the state's authority: the authority of God at least transcends it, and may indeed be in principle in direct conflict with it. What is remarkable from the point of view of our present concern is how little direct interest there is anywhere in ethical questions raised by life in relation to political authority. Even what there is works obliquely and as a by-product of more pressing motives.

But there remains one thing to be said. Even if the critique of secular political authority was minimal and was nowhere directed to detailed matters of structure or practice, early Christians put forward radical ideas about the structure of power within the Church itself, which, whether by way of affirmation or neglect or denial, had a momentous future ahead of them. On the basis of the slave-like self-giving of Jesus, service is to be the distinguishing mark of those who have authority in the christian body – and with this an ideal presented itself capable of extension in due course from the ecclesiastical to the political sphere in christian states (cf. Mark x, 42–5; Luke xxii, 25–7; John xiii, 12–15). This ideal is applied to the apostle by Paul (II Cor. iv, 5), but the natural development of more formal structure in the Church rapidly led to its sharp edge being blunted. Early in the second century, Ignatius, leader of the church in Antioch, was already able to present a picture of the christian ministry, whereby the bishop represented God the Father (the 'authority-figure'), while it was left to the deacons to stand for Jesus – and so the paradox of the leader/servant was lost.[8]

(iii) WEALTH

Did the early Church feel a need to formulate teaching about problems arising from the possession of wealth? Was there any sense that christian faith and life were incompatible with either more than a modest amount of property or any

8. See M. Staniforth (ed.), *Early Christian Writings* (Penguin, 1968), pp. 88, 95f.

private property at all? If so, by what routes was the logic worked out?

One thing is clear: the New Testament is fairly thickly dotted with attacks on the rich. It appears that no New Testament writer had much time for the possessors of wealth, and few of them refrained from expressing their antagonism. This consensus is significant in itself. Wealth aroused the ire of early Christians with ease. But what objections did they have? After all, people attack the rich for many reasons which have little to do with ethics.

The Epistle of James (i, 9–11; ii, 1–7; v, 1–6) expresses the most straightforward view of all, at considerable length. The wealthy are callous, fraudulent and oppressive. The day of reckoning is on the way. They are to be shown no special deference, and they ought to be glad if they lose their property, for that will give them the chance to learn how transient possessions are. Some of this doctrine (especially ii, 5) is close to being inverted snobbery at its simplest – an outburst of 'have nots' against the 'haves'. But it echoes well-worn themes of Old Testament religion; it is part of the conventional language of piety (cf. Psalm xlix, 16ff.; Isaiah v, 8–10).

The idea that poverty is pleasing to God and in itself gives a man a head-start in the devout life continued to be current in Judaism in the period of the New Testament. It is found, especially in the form of the abandonment of private in favour of communal ownership, in the sect of Qumran;[9] it is found in the very title of the later jewish christian sect of the 'Ebionites' (the Poor). It is prominent in several New Testament writers: Luke vi, 20; Matthew v, 3, where the

9. See G. Vermes, *The Dead Sea Scrolls in English* (Penguin, 1962). pp. 29f., 240; compare the use of the term 'poverty' in this sense in christian monasticism.

expression 'poor in spirit' perhaps explicitly makes the link between poverty of life and the piety of the heart. Not surprisingly, then, it is a great scandal for a christian congregation to be wealthy (Rev. iii, 17). Not that extreme poverty, such as that of a significant proportion of the primitive Jerusalem church (Gal. ii, 10; cf. Acts vi), was always to be admired or embraced. The writer of I Timothy urges contentment with a modest sufficiency (vi, 6–10) and knows the dangers to the faith of those who develop a craving for more.

That craving is castigated by Luke (e.g. xii, 15–21), for whom, as we have seen (p. 57), generosity is the heart of virtue and close-fistedness and attachment to possessions are the greatest of sins. He goes on to show (note 'Therefore' in xii, 22) that anxiety about the things of this life is wrong because it is an expression of this attachment. (Matthew in the parallel passage (vi, 25–33) gives more emphasis than Luke to the fact that anxiety also betrays a failure in single-minded adherence to God's service, cf. vi, 19–24, and cf. his commendation of almsgiving provided it is done with purity of motive, vi, 2–4.) The solution is to give alms freely (Luke xii, 32–4) – that will bring possession of the kingdom, by the Father's gift. For Luke riches are the great obstacle to the christian life, for 'you cannot serve God and mammon' (xvi, 13 and Matt. vi, 24).

Mark, characteristically, had placed this teaching on the theological plane. The trouble with riches lay not fundamentally in the moral weakness to which they gave rise but in the impediment they create to the wholeheartedness of a man's acceptance of God's rule (presumably, by giving him another object of trust). They prevent him from entering the kingdom (x, 17–27). Observance of the moral law has to be transcended by unfettered attachment to Jesus. This renunciation and attachment brings its own new wealth (x, 28–31) – the fellowship and resources of the christian community here and now (changed by Matthew into a purely future, heavenly compensation for stringency on earth).

Matthew (xix, 16–30) makes several alterations in this passage (apart from that just noted). He makes a distinction between 'entering into life' (verse 17), to be achieved by keeping the Decalogue, and 'being perfect' (verse 21), to be achieved only by the abandonment of all possessions. This may indicate that he accepted two grades of christian discipleship in the Church, one more strenuous than the other. Certainly, the apparently general application of the command to 'be perfect' in v. 48 tells against this, but if the distinction is intentional, expressing Matthew's practical and organizing mind, then it is in sharp contrast with both Mark's theological approach and Luke's clear insistence on the need for all Christians to be ready to undertake this sacrifice and to live generously.

Paul urges generosity within the christian body, basing his exhortation on Christ's self-giving (II Cor. viii, 9), and on a sense of the flow of benefits within the Church (Rom. xv, 25–7). These motives make his collection for the church in Jerusalem (cf. also Gal. ii, 10 and I Cor. xvi, 1) more than a merely financial exercise. It has a deep sacramental significance, for it represents the unity in Christ of jewish and gentile Christians.

John is silent on the responsibilities of property. He refers to the duty of generosity to the poor only to say that it is suspended in the crisis of Christ's passion (xii, 5–8; but cf. xiii, 29). It is John's solitary, momentary recognition of duty to the needs of society at large. Is it possibly a symptom of more, to which the tightness of John's theological pattern and purpose did not allow expression in his book?

The First Epistle of John interprets the command to love one's brothers in terms of providing for their needs (iii, 11–18), and the Gospel shows the disciples, who received the command to love one another, sharing a common purse (John xii, 6; xiii, 29).

(iv) TOLERATION

Though it would be anachronistic to suggest that 'toleration' ever posed itself as an issue in the early Church, the congregations of the first century did have to decide what limits to draw to their doctrinal and religious sympathies. They arrived at their decisions within the wide frame of the Roman Empire and the narrower one of Judaism. The former provided an example of wide tolerance in matters of both belief and practice (cf. p. 85), saving always the safety of the state – including adherence to the official cults whereby that safety was divinely assured. In Judaism too, within a strong sense of exclusiveness over against all other faiths (which were both false and idolatrous), there was more room for manoeuvre than has often been supposed, both in doctrine and in religious observance. The former could range from the stark conservatism of the Sadducees to the modified Platonism of Philo of Alexandria; while observance diverged considerably among the sects (Pharisees, Sadducees, Essenes and Zealots), all of which nevertheless preserved certain fixed points of practice like circumcision and the sabbath. In this situation, while there was naturally great pressure within the Church to follow the narrow exclusiveness of Judaism whose heir it felt itself to be, there was also sufficient breadth of tolerance in the air (even the jewish air) for it to be possible for the balance to tilt in that direction.

When we come to examine the attitudes taken up in relation to this matter by the early Church, we find amazing diversity – almost as wide as could possibly have been without the new faith dissolving away and losing its identity. This is true in relation to both gentile and jewish culture.

First in relation to the culture and religions of the Empire. It is hard to suppose that the writer of the Revelation to John exercised much fine discrimination between good and bad in the life of the Roman imperial order. Under the figure of the whore of Babylon, he presented it as the incarnation of evil, wholly in opposition to God (Rev. xvii). But this is not the message of other New Testament writers. Paul, for example, gave a measure of both explicit and implicit approval at least to the ethical ideals and concepts of pagan society. It is explicit in his remarks about the universal moral consciousness of man (Rom. ii, 14f.), and implicit in his straightforward and almost unmodified adoption of conventional pagan lists of virtues and vices, of the terms of current (especially stoic) ethics, and of catalogues of household duties (I Cor. vi, 9f.; Col. iii, 18ff.; cf. Eph, v, 22–vi, 9; I Peter ii, 18–iii, 7; see p. 32). He shows no awareness of formally reaching out to use foreign resources, but on the contrary gives every impression of simply accepting these elements as part of the common air which all men breathe. Nor does he show awareness of any cleavage between this, the accepted morality of his day, and his innovations, where the christian gospel calls the tune. Examples of the latter are the argument against fornication in I Corinthians vi, 13 – 'the body is meant . . . for the Lord' – and above all the hymn in exploration of the meaning of love in I Corinthians xiii.

Paul also believes in at least the possibility of pagans seeing the basic truth about God: 'God has shown it to them' (Rom. i, 19f.). And Luke, with his apologetic stance, can say the same in his portrayal of Paul in the speech at Athens (Acts xvii, 28). This common ground is the basis of Paul's appeal against pagan idolatry and for conversion to the true God.

The question arises whether Paul, so firm against polytheism and false worship, nevertheless imported into Christianity elements from pagan religion, in particular from the mystery cults, even to the extent of inconsistency with central features of the Church's gospel. It is in principle a very hard question because 'the gospel' has, to our sight, only the most shadowy of shapes and the flimsiest of clothing before Paul. Still, there could clearly be elements which did violence to the heart of the christian message. Few critics would now hold that his teaching about baptism and the Eucharist to any large degree depends on the inspiration of roughly comparable rites in the pagan mysteries. Nevertheless, there are features both of these rites (cf. his own comparison-cum-contrast in I Corinthians x, 21, for example) and of other Pauline concepts (such as his distinction between 'spiritual' and other, less advanced Christians in I Corinthians ii, 14ff.) which probably owe something to these sources. Here again, there is no sign that Paul is consciously borrowing foreign goods, and it is hard to say how far he deliberately uses the terms of pagan religion in order to tame them for christian use by setting them in the context of the gospel.[10]

A similar problem arises in relation to alleged Platonism in the Fourth Gospel and, to a lesser degree, in the Epistle to the Hebrews. It is almost certain that in so far as this is an important feature in the background to these writings, it does not arise from a positive strategy of intellectual assimilation. To these writers (and it is doubtful whether in either case anything as sophisticated as a formal philosophy was

10. See H. Chadwick, 'All things to all men', *New Testament Studies*, Vol. 1, 1955.

really influential), this was the way to regard the universe and the setting in which the gospel must naturally be expressed.

In relation to Judaism, again there was a wide range of reactions. We have already seen something of the New Testament writers' varied attitudes to the Law (cf. especially pp. 80ff.), but on the broader issue too there was no single approach. Judaism was undeniably the parent of the Church, and love and hate mingled inextricably. Certainly neither Paul nor Matthew nor even John succeeded in severing the cord that bound child to mother. The Epistle to the Ephesians, almost certainly the work of an imitator and devotee of Paul in the following generation, is perhaps the first writing which can look back on the Church's roots in Judaism without hostility and with some detachment: the Christians are a third entity, reconciling Jew and Gentile into the 'one new Man' (ii, 11ff.). But no New Testament writer fails to recognize that even though Jesus is the centre of all that spells salvation and true life, nevertheless in important senses 'salvation is from the Jews' (John iv, 22).

However, sometimes there is more toleration, sometimes less. Matthew (xxiii) has little good to say of the dominant pharisaic Judaism of his day, towards the end of the first century. For John, 'the Jews' are the enemies of Christ, yet not wholly so (viii, 31), and it is hard to tell how far they are simply a 'stage crowd', the representatives of sinful mankind. Perhaps this gospel reflects a milieu where the christian claims gave rise to varied reactions among Jews (vii, 40f.). Despite his share in producing the crescendo with which the successive gospels intensify the responsibility of the jewish authorities for Christ's death, Luke shows much less hostility to Judaism in itself and to the Jews as a people: there is in his presentation a gentle emergence of the Church from Judaism rather than a fresh beginning (cf. pp. 61f.); Paul himself never makes a clean break in Luke's story of him, and both priests and Pharisees are converts to the new faith (Acts vi, 7; xv, 5; cf. Luke xxiii, 50; Acts v, 34f.). Like the author of Ephesians, Luke finds a degree of detachment possible. Colossians may reflect a situation where relations between Christians and Jews are those of amicable discussion rather than bitter controversy.[11]

One problem which raised the issue of toleration acutely for many early Christians was that of food taboos. There was a whole cluster of questions: should Jews eat with Gentiles when both were Christians? should gentile converts to the Church keep the jewish food laws? should Christians eat meat from the pagan butchers' shops, knowing much of it to have been technically offered in the pagan temples, or refuse as Jews would refuse?[12] It is clear that in the lifetime of Paul, the Jerusalem Church (which disappeared in the fall of the city in A.D. 70, before any of the other New Testament books, apart from Paul's letters, are likely to have seen the light of day) found it extremely difficult to exercise tolerance in this matter, whether out of conviction or out of apprehensiveness concerning the reaction of Jews among whom they, unlike Paul, had to live and whom they hoped to evangelize. For them there was little pressure to adopt a liberal attitude on the question, but for Paul, amid his gentile converts, table fellowship among Christians was a touchstone of faith, as his reaction to Peter's vacillation in the matter shows (Gal. ii, 11ff.). It sprang straight from the unity of all in Christ, the new Adam (I Cor. xii, 13; xv, 22; Gal. iii, 28).

11. See J. L. Houlden, *Paul's Letters from Prison* (Penguin, 1970), pp. 128f.
12. See W. Schmithals, *Paul and James* (London, 1965); C. K. Barrett, 'Things sacrificed to idols', *New Testament Studies*, Vol. ii, 1965.

On the matter of eating food that had been offered to idols, his attitude shows great width of sympathy – and it was based not on expediency but on a combination of deep theological principles and the duty of considerate love. The argument appears at its fullest in I Corinthians viii–x, more briefly in Romans xiv. The general situation is clear: Paul has moved so far from adherence to the Law that tolerance no longer need be extended to those who wish to abrogate the food taboos but to those who wish to retain them, that is Christians of tender conscience, whether Jews converted to the Church or gentile Christians who value the exclusiveness of their new faith. The food laws no longer hold for a number of reasons: because 'the earth is the Lord's and everything in it' (I Cor. x, 26); or else because thanks is due to God for all food, and to give thanks is to justify the eating (I Cor. x, 30f.); or again, this is not what Christians are to concern themselves with – 'the kingdom of God does not mean food and drink but righteousness and peace and joy in the Holy Spirit' (Rom. xiv, 17); and in any case, Paul feels inspired by the risen Jesus to believe (or knows a tradition of his teaching to this effect) that 'nothing is unclean in itself' (Rom. xiv, 14). Nevertheless, despite this array of arguments, the consciences of weaker brethren are to be scrupulously respected.

Paul's tolerant doctrine about food appears also in Jesus' teaching in Mark (vii, 19). Matthew omits the crucial phrase ('thus he declared all foods clean') in accordance with his generally conservative attitude to the Law. Luke omits from his Gospel the incident in which this issue is raised, but settles it in the Markan sense in Acts x, where verse 15 may mean that the taboos had always been an error. Nevertheless, Acts xv, 20 decrees that gentile Christians, like jewish Christians, are to abstain from food that has been offered to idols: within the general permission, gentile converts are to make this gesture of peace and compromise (in typically Lukan manner). This act probably has theological meaning too (cf. p. 61).

To judge from the New Testament, the question of circumcising gentile converts seems to have been settled early, in the liberal sense, and to have caused no further interest. Thus Paul had to fight for his policy – he even seems to have considered it obsolete for jewish Christians (such is the logic of Galatians v) – but clearly he won the battle (Gal. ii, 3), and the issue makes no appearance whatsoever in the gospels. It looks as if it was dead by the time they came to be written.[13] Even the jewish christian Gospel of Matthew makes no mention of it: baptism is firmly the rite of initiation for Christians (xxviii, 19) and has replaced the old jewish rite. Only in Acts xv, where gentile converts are relieved of the need to undergo the rite (verses 1–5, 10), and in xvi, 3 does it come into Luke's account of the early Church. This incident, in which the benefit of the doubt is given in favour of circumcision in the case of a child of mixed parentage, may well be included partly to compensate for the liberal ruling of the council in chapter xv and partly as one element in the portrayal of Paul as the non-extremist on the issue of the Law (cf. p. 61). It may even be meant to soften the effect of the incident concerning Titus (a converted Greek whom Paul refused to subject to the jewish rite) recorded in Paul's own Epistle to the Galatians (ii, 3). It contributes then to Luke's picture of the early Church as a community essentially harmonious and conciliatory in its

13. This view insists upon the fact that the gospels are products of the late-first-century Church and reflect primarily the interests of that time. Those who hold that they reflect no less those of Jesus' lifetime will point out that circumcision only began to be an issue once the mission to Gentiles had got under way, so that its absence from the gospels causes no surprise.

treatment of the differences between its jewish and gentile members.

As far as the circumcision of Jesus himself is concerned, Luke alone tells of it (ii, 21), in a spirit of simple piety. Like the whole of his narrative of Jesus' birth (chapters i–ii), this act shows Jesus' roots amongst the devout people of old Israel. For positive theological reflection, we turn from the New Testament to the collect for the feast dedicated to the circumcision of the Lord in the Book of Common Prayer: he 'was obedient to the law for man'.

An attitude of tolerance on many matters, depending on a variety of reasons, did not inhibit the early congregations from exercising discipline among their members. Paul decrees that the immoral Christian is to be excluded from fellowship, though in a spirit of hope for his ultimate salvation: the exclusion is, partly at least, purgative (I Cor. v). Matthew too sees a place for the exclusion of the obstinate by properly constituted church authority (xviii, 15–19; cf. xxii, 11–14). The Epistle to the Hebrews is so conscious of the splendour of the transition effected by becoming a Christian that subsequent apostasy can meet no mercy – a second chance is impossible (vi, 4–6).

These are all instances of the disciplining of Christians who failed to meet the community's demands. It seems that the lines could be tightly drawn – though there were signs of a greater understanding of human frailty, especially in private dealings (Matt. xviii, 21f.; Luke xvii, 3f.). It was a matter of discovering how God's forgiveness, on which all depended, could be reflected in the life of the Church, without dissolution into scandalous anarchy (Luke xv, 11ff.; Matt. xviii, 23ff.).

On doctrinal issues, there are signs of hardening as the period covered by the New Testament nears its end. Paul gives no hint of wishing to exclude from the community those in his congregations whose beliefs he holds to be erroneous. It was not to remain so for long. By the time of John's first epistle, Christians were capable of going formally into schism and excommunicating others (ii, 19). And in I Timothy i, 19f., the discipline which Paul exercised in an ethical matter is used in a case of aberrant teaching. So the course was set for the future, when from the second century rival groups of Christians came to face one another without a trace of tolerance, and 'orthodoxy' and 'heresy' are labels that can be attached to distinct communities.

How tolerant were the first Christians of pagan religious belief? At first sight, not at all: they were as firmly monotheist as the Jews. But the very *élan* with which they held to the triumph of Jesus, the one from God, led to a tendency to brush aside or absorb the pagan deities rather than simply oppose them. Paul is ambiguous. The deities have no real existence, or if they have, that existence entirely depends on Christ through whom they came into being and by whom they have been brought into subjection (I Cor. viii, 4–6; Col. i, 15–20). Or else the gods are demons in disguise (I Cor. x, 19–21); when this idea is uppermost, Paul's tone is sharper.

Already then, in the New Testament, we meet that combination of exclusiveness and adaptability which was a major factor in the Church's ultimate triumph in the Roman Empire. The adaptability was largely unconscious, and perhaps only this made it persist as a feature of christian thought and teaching. And, with whatever nuances, the exclusiveness was absolute and severe: 'for although there may be so-called gods in heaven or on earth – as indeed there are many "gods" and many "lords" – yet for us there is one God, the Father, from whom are all things and for whom we exist, and one Lord, Jesus Christ, through whom are all things and through whom we exist' (I Cor. viii, 5f.).

4. The Lord

BEHIND the writers and behind the Church which formed them stood Jesus. We have seen the diversity of teaching which had arisen within a few decades of his ministry, and the forces which prompted this vigorous growth. We have examined the variety of solutions which early congregations worked out for some of the moral problems confronting them, and noted the range of sources from which they derived their moral convictions – from the conventional assumptions of contemporary society (jewish or pagan) to demands springing directly from their own christian belief. The variety was largely unconscious: no New Testament writer, except James in relation to Paul (James ii, 14f.), shows himself aware that other Christians thought in terms other than his own. Even Matthew, altering Mark as he used him, probably saw himself as bringing out the earlier writer's 'true' sense.

All have their root in Jesus, in one way or another. The appeal is explicit in the case of the evangelists, and it appears in direct form momentarily in Paul's ethical teaching (I Cor. vii, 10; ix, 14; xiv, 37). Jesus taught and these writers ostensibly reproduce his teaching. Their work, and its speedy popularity, is evidence of how important the direct authority of Jesus in these, as in other, matters was soon felt to be, at least by some Christians. But their presentations of his teaching differ and are even incompatible, both in detail and in total concept. Moreover, other christian writers give ethical teaching which either has its roots in Jesus in a much more complex way or (if it is commonplace morality and receives no doctrinal basis) has no clear roots in him at all (cf. p. 64).

To bring out these facts, we have called this chapter not 'Jesus' but 'the Lord'. The title reflects the complexity of his role. For all the early congregations whose teaching is before us in the New Testament, Jesus was not only (even primarily) a figure of the past, but the present Lord who ruled and inspired their common life, and who was soon to return in glory, as king and judge of all. Whenever this consciousness was strong, ethical teaching appeared as issuing from his authority, however it was expressed. Sometimes it was the merest veneer on the surface of unquestioned conventional values; servants were to obey their masters and children their parents, but with the rider 'fearing the Lord' (Col. iii, 22) or 'for this pleases the Lord' (Col. iii, 20). Sometimes an aspect of Jesus' life or death was to be the model for christian conduct, e.g. humility, for Christ 'emptied himself, taking the form of a servant' (Phil. ii, 4ff.). Or else his general example stood as the power behind christian moral life: 'as I have loved you, that you also love one another' (John xiii, 34).

Jesus was both the present Lord and the past inaugurator. He was the fount of the process whose development we see in the New Testament and the Church. But how much did the fount contribute to the stream, and how much came from tributaries running into it from the circumstances of Church life and from the surrounding culture? And how far did the resulting mixture become one in which the twin roles of Jesus the Lord, as inaugurator in the past and as inspirer of the Church's present life, could no longer be readily distinguished? In Paul, there are traces of awareness that such a distinction may be made: there are matters on which the apostle has a tradition of Jesus' teaching and matters on which he has not (I Cor. vii, 10, 12, 25). But development is on the way. Paul's teaching in matters where that of Jesus is not available is not mere opinion, for he thinks he is possessed by the Spirit of God (I Cor. vii, 40). In I Corinthians ii he unfolds the seriousness with which he sees this inspiration. It is a veritable occupation of a Christian's thinking by God; and moreover the indwelling by the Spirit can be equally well described as possessing the mind of Christ (verse 16). In the Spirit-laden atmosphere of many of the early congregations, it is no great distance from 'the Lord now says' to 'Jesus said'; from the present statement, Lo, I come as a thief! Blessed is he who is awake' (Rev. xvi, 15), to the use of this figure and theme (in a different form) by the Jesus of the past (Matt. xxiv, 43). (It is possible of course that the two instances of this language arose independently or that the influence worked in the opposite direction; the general point remains.)

After Paul, it is not impossible that the distinction, already blurring, was often obliterated, so that we cannot be sure whether teaching ascribed to Jesus in the gospels, written twenty to fifty years after Paul's letters, is his own or arose in the early Church. Paul teaches submission to rulers without mentioning Jesus' teaching on the matter (Rom. xiii, 1ff.); the gospels ascribe such teaching to Jesus (Mark xii, 13–17). Was Paul taking Jesus' teaching for granted, or was he unaware of it as he formulated his own? Or did teaching like Paul's come to be seen as authorized first by the living Lord, then finally by the Jesus of history?

The ambiguity in the term 'the Lord' may be expressed in another way. By the time any of our writings appeared he was both the source of a body of teaching and the object of religious allegiance, the one who had taught and the one who had died and been raised. Again, by the time the gospels were written, the day had long passed (had it ever been, for anything that can be called *christian* faith?) when it was possible to distinguish the two. This is not to say that the gospels contain no authentic teaching from Jesus; it is to say that that teaching is seen as that of one who is the object of faith and this could not fail to colour the presentation of the tradition of his words, whether deeply or otherwise. Moreover, that faith itself is 'shaped' differently in each of the four gospels. When we examined their ethical teaching we found in each case a distinct theological and religious approach. This adds a further factor which makes it difficult if not impossible for us to affirm with certainty at any particular point that we meet the teaching of Jesus as distinct from the evangelist's response to him, both as a figure of the past and as the present Lord.

Moreover, in our account of the moral teaching of the evangelists, we have paid them the compliment of believing that they understood and meant what they wrote! It is possible of course that they accepted sayings of Jesus from the tradition and reproduced them out of mere faithfulness, even when their personal standpoint would not readily have admitted such words, or although they themselves might have chosen to express the matter otherwise. Many books about the gospels, which lay little emphasis on the evangelists' own thought, accept that they derived more or less of their material from good tradition, while omitting to consider the application of this negative test: could, for example, Matthew, being the man he was, willingly have expressed himself thus? If not, are we not one stage nearer the presence of authentic tradition? In fact, though our survey has been far from exhaustive, we have seen reason to think that the gospels present in all four cases coherent pictures of Jesus' teaching. We have seen that they differ from each other in their version of a particular story or saying precisely where, on the ground of their general standpoint, we should expect. The more this is found to be the case, the more hazardous becomes the search for what Jesus really taught; though there is no logic which could lead us to believe that of four accounts of a man's teaching all are equally remote from the truth or that, even if all four express distinctive views of him, he is thereby rendered totally obscure to us. It may be that he did not speak precisely so and so, but that nevertheless the thrust of his message was thus and thus.

If we turn from the figure of Jesus to the Church's message, we find a corresponding ambiguity. In Paul, that message ('the gospel') was concerned with Jesus, the crucified and risen Lord. But in the gospels, where he is presented overall as the one who is *now* crucified and risen, the dominant message is that of the preaching and deeds of Jesus, and the concern is with the nearness of the Kingdom of God and the consequent demand for repentance. (The word 'gospel' itself is used unambiguously in this sense by Matthew, as is clear from his addition of the words 'of the kingdom' (e.g. iv, 23) to the unqualified use of the word in Mark. In Mark it is generally unclear which of the two 'messages' is chiefly meant, that of the Church's faith, concerning Jesus, or that of Jesus, concerning the Kingdom, e.g. i, 1, 15; viii, 34.) Though this interest in the message *of* Jesus, as distinct from the message *concerning* Jesus, makes a relatively late literary appearance, and is notoriously lacking in Paul, the earliest source, it would be surprising if it had not been continuous from the first days. Thus, even though Paul, perhaps largely as a result of his dominant theological patterns, shows little direct interest in the historical Jesus, he must have known enough about him to justify his persecuting zeal (Gal. i, 13). Certainly, interest in Jesus' own message and teaching must have experienced a vigorous revival for the writing of the books about him to take place.

Both ways of conceiving the christian message – and it is likely that they co-existed in many churches, as the portrayal of Jesus as both teacher and Lord shows –

shared one feature of central significance in the development of early christian ethics: a critique of the jewish Law. Jesus' own preaching challenged it, and so did the Church which proclaimed him as Lord. For the churches of the first century (unless they had no contact with Jews either in their own membership or in their neighbourhood), the moral issue – the issue of obedience to God, both in principle and in detail – crystallized round the Law. It stood as an already existing moral guide, vast in prestige and scope, the gift of God. Whatever other sources of moral thinking he might tap, no christian moralist could avoid coming to terms with it. All of those we know from the New Testament had in one way or another to use it as a reference point, even a *point de départ*.

The critique took two forms: of the Law as a religious principle, and of the Law as a code of ethics. The first form of the critique was pre-eminently the work of Paul, and was conducted in terms of faith. Concerned with man's acceptance by God, Paul saw it as impossible on the basis of obedience to the Law, and available only through attachment, by God's sheer grace, to Jesus Christ. This critique, explicit in Paul, is implicit in the gospels (and indeed in all the New Testament writers), for Jesus is now the religious 'centre' – the one through whom alone the true relationship with God is to be found. In the Gospel of John, indeed, there is a considerable degree of application to Jesus of images hitherto associated with the Law, which he now replaces as the route to and from God (e.g. bread of life, truth, word, way).

The second form of the critique, found both in Paul and in the gospels, is in terms of love. It is no longer the case, except for Matthew and probably James, that the whole Law remains binding on Christians: discrimination is possible. Among the rabbis, the opinion was current that to avoid treating one's neighbour in a way in which one would not like to be treated oneself was the quintessence of the Law – every item of which was nevertheless vital.[1] Matthew accepts this view (xxii, 40; vii, 12), but sharpens its impact further by the stringent commands which express the greater righteousness now required by Jesus (v, 20–48), and by interpreting the Law, always in firm scriptural argument (cf. his use of Hosea vi, 6 in ix, 13 and xii, 7), in accordance with the love command. The other evangelists and Paul are clearer in giving pride of place to the command to love (cf. p. 72). This is henceforth the overriding moral requirement and by it the Law is not merely newly interpreted but rivalled and supplanted. Not only is the principle accepted of grading moral rules according to importance and centrality, but the idea now emerges, especially in John (cf. p. 36), that provided this command is kept, summing up the spirit of the Law, the rest may be dropped from sight.[2]

The critique of the Law both exemplifies the distinction between the twin forms of the gospel and bridges the gap. Jesus the Lord was the means whereby the Law could be superseded as a religious force. Jesus in his lifetime is presented as teaching the radical reinterpretation of the Law, whether by intensifying its central commands (as in Matthew), or by abandoning some of its most precious provisions, like the rigour of sabbath observance (as in the other evangelists). In word and in person, he calls the Law into question. Though from a literary point of view we have

1. D. E. Nineham, *Gospel of Saint Mark* (Pelican, 1963), p. 324.
2. For the sabbath law John has an ingenious critique of his own. The sabbath represents God's rest after his activity in creation. But which now characterizes God's life, activity or rest? Life-giving activity, says John. Jesus manifests God, so he too is active, and where life is to be bestowed, sabbath goes by the board. All of which is lost on the Jews who do not dwell in the light. See John v, 9b, 16–18; cf. vii, 22f.; ix, 14–16.

older evidence of the 'faith' critique, based on Jesus the pres
ent Lord, than of the 'love' critique, based on Jesus the
teacher, it is hard to believe that in some form the latter was
not a crucial part of his message and indeed close to the
heart of the offence for which official Judaism brough
about his condemnation; hard to believe that he did no
teach that which he was later seen to have exemplified.

The two forms of the critique are joined in a second way
The 'faith' critique raises the question: what is it about Jesus
which arouses this decisive response? In Paul, the answer i
provided only in theological terms: Jesus has this role be
cause of his identity – he is 'the Son', the one whom God sen
(Rom. viii, 3) and 'gave up for us all' (Rom. viii, 32). There is
no hint that the role depends in any way on features of the
character or teaching of the historical Jesus. Not merely i
there no feeling that Jesus 'merited' this role by his manne
of life, it is not even suggested that his behaviour was con
sistent with it (except conceivably in Philippians ii, 6–11
though even here it is a question less of his moral qualitie
than of the drama in which he had engaged). With the evan
gelists the case is necessarily different. For Luke, Jesus no
only gives strong moral teaching, but also himsel
exemplifies it, and even at his death he practises generous
kindness and forgiveness (Luke xxiii, 28–31, 34, 39–43). His
moral authority receives grounding in his own human con
duct. Similarly for Matthew, Jesus is the one who welcomes
encourages and reassures his disciples as well as teaching
them (vi, 25–34; xi, 25–30; xxviii, 16–20). John portrays
Jesus as the one who, above all in his hour of trial, shows
love for his own (xiii, 1–35). Only in Mark, with the portrai
of Jesus as the enigmatic agent of God who meets the rebuff
and opposition of all, is there a figure of conflict rather than
of compassion, one about whom theological statements can
be made rather than an authority for ethics; though even

Mark's Jesus draws men to follow him and commands them to love God and their neighbour.

The gospels then by their portrayal of Jesus face and answer the question of linking the two forms of the critique. Jesus is the object of faith, in that he displays qualities which attract men's deepest allegiance and inspire their discipleship. Thus faith itself gives rise, because of Jesus, to the predominance of love in ethics. Attachment merges into obedience and imitation. The cross above all is not only the focus of salvation and release but also of ethical example, especially for Luke.

It is now time to formulate the question: what was the ethical teaching of Jesus, or, more modestly, what is the most reasonable conjecture that we can make? One fundamental matter has already come before us. We felt justified in saying that even taking the most sceptical view of the historicity of the gospels, surely Jesus must have initiated the critique of the Law, whether or not he did it precisely as the gospels show. Though in principle all the relevant material could have been read back into Jesus' lifetime in the light of the Church's opposition to the Law (originally on Pauline grounds, which have no need of Jesus' *teaching* for their force), if this were so, it would be hard to understand the hostility aroused by Jesus; and the great degree of acceptance accorded to Paul by the Jerusalem apostles (Gal. ii, 1–10) makes it unlikely that he was wholly an innovator in this crucial respect.

In the search for an answer to our question, the reason for the hostility to Jesus is one of the most important avenues open to us. The accounts in the gospels show Jesus' death to have been the result of Jewish opposition to his work. The execution was carried out by the Roman authorities because they alone had the power to do it, and they were only persuaded to carry it out because the jewish leaders made Jesus out to be a political danger. As is well known, it has been argued that this version of the story arose from the desire of the Church of the second half of the first century to convince the Roman government of its harmlessness and as a projection of its own bitter controversies with Jews in various parts of the Empire. In reality, Jesus had been executed by Pontius Pilate because he was seen as a political threat – his movement had much in common with the nationalist Zealots – and the picture of the pacific Christ is simply one element in the evangelists' apologetic. This is no place to argue for the general accuracy of the gospels' account. It must suffice to say that the evidence against it remains unconvincing. Though it is true that the gospels bear witness to a mounting tendency in the early Church to place the blame for Jesus' death on the Jews, the rise and survival of the christian movement in the form we see in the New Testament is hard to explain except in terms of the traditional picture. Moreover, the detailed evidence, when looked at either from the point of view of historical scholarship or from the standpoint of literary method, seems to tell in the same direction.[3] We take it that Jesus was opposed and executed for his teaching on questions related to jewish religious belief. At a time when strict orthodoxy was not rigidly insisted upon (cf. p. 92), Jesus went beyond the pale. Our question then is: what is that teaching likely to have been?

We may find another clue if we attempt to answer the question: what was Jesus' relationship to the current eschatological hopes of so many Jews? If anything is clear about the preaching of Jesus, it is that he preached the urgent approach of the breaking in of God's lordship over

3. See S. G. F. Brandon, *The Trial of Jesus of Nazareth* (London, 1968), with review by A. N. Sherwin-White in *Gnomon*, 1971; and E. Bammel (ed.), *The Trial of Jesus* (London, 1970).

the world. Whatever the precise form that it took, it was the excitement of this message which gave the fundamental impetus to Jesus and those who followed him.

If we put together these two strands – that his offence was against the religious assumptions of a not particularly intolerant Judaism and that his preaching was eschatological in standpoint through and through – are we able to be more precise about our contention that Jesus must lie behind that critique of the Law which is so prominent in the New Testament and in the early Church? Kurt Niederwimmer, in his *Jesus* (Göttingen, 1968), maintains that it is not satisfactory to suppose that Jesus was unusual merely through reinterpreting the Law, as Matthew's broad presentation of him suggests (cf. p. 49). To have worked thus within the confines of the rabbinic and scribal 'game' would not have brought condemnation, and would have been unlikely to lead to the new movement which Jesus initiated so forcefully. Rather, 'Jesus stands over against the whole sacred tradition of his people, the written as well as the oral, with an astonishing sovereign independence and inner freedom.'[4] Jesus has removed himself from the aegis of the Law altogether, taking parts of it and refusing others as seems right – in the light of God's overwhelming lordship.

Such a view of Jesus' radicalism certainly accounts for the deep opposition which he aroused: he was accepting the implications of God's sovereignty so seriously that he found himself, for God's sake, breaking right out of the assumptions within which the jewish religion conducted itself. Such a view also accounts for the powerful and distinctive effect of his life and death, which Niederwimmer can describe as a sacrifice for the radical standpoint which he adopted. And it accounts for the persistent prominence of

4. Op. cit., p. 55, my translation.

the non-legal love-command, in so many and such different elements in the New Testament.

It is not surprising, on this view, that there is no early tradition of Jesus' having given a fully worked out moral or ritual code (his approach was essentially lay rather than clerical). Rather, he makes vivid gestures from which men are to draw their conclusions – a healing, a striking saying, the Last Supper, and in a manner, the crucifixion itself.[5] By the time the books came to be written, Jesus was already being edged into the role of the giver of a revised law for his people. It appears even in John, least law-ridden of gospels, in the new *commandment* of xiii, 34. It appears most obviously in the arguments based on the jewish Law which give so many of Jesus' acts their authority in the Gospel of Matthew. Yet even in Matthew, Jesus' teaching (e.g. in v, 21–48) is such as to transcend the level of law: these commands cannot be kept in the way that a law needs to be capable of being kept. Even within the Matthean framework, which at least partly sets out to present Jesus as a new Moses, mediating the new commands to his people, the implications of God's urgent lordship are maintained, whether the precise formulation goes back to Jesus or not.

Jesus' freedom with regard to the Law manifests itself not only in what appears to be sheer rigorism (when viewed apart from the sense of God's immediacy and power, which is its correct context), but also, by contrast, in apparent laxity – Jesus, gentleness with sinners and the constant motif of his associating with the outcasts of society. He was, says Niederwimmer, 'a friend of the enemies of Yahweh', of those disqualified by the rules of the Law. Jesus depicts God not as the father of his obedient sons, but rather of the disobedient. Only this message of forgiveness, of the removal of burdens from men's shoulders, can have made 'good news'

5. See H. A. Williams, *True Resurrection* (London, 1972), pp. 116ff.

the term which, in at least some christian circles, seemed most appropriate for what they had found. To make the picture of Jesus credible in the light of what sprang from him, his teaching must have been an ethic not merely of rigorous commands but equally a message of salvation: if that teaching had not already in his lifetime been a message of hope, would not the resurrection faith have lacked foundations on which to build? It is hard to believe that the character of that faith was wholly spontaneous at Easter. Moreover, his teaching must have had the most intimate bond with his own behaviour: the nature of the link is lost to us, but without it his authority is incredible, and again Easter has to bear too great a burden of innovation.[6]

Undoubtedly, gospel sayings can be produced to illustrate every aspect of Jesus' teaching to which we have referred. In that teaching the proclamation of the Kingdom is hard to distinguish from the arrow-like statements about human life and behaviour to which the proclamation gives rise. Some of the statements have every air of authenticity, yet in chapter 2 we used many of them as evidence for the teaching of one or another of the evangelists. Are we then committing ourselves to the view that Jesus spoke in the tones of more than one of the gospels, or that the standpoints of the evangelists are less distinctive than we suggested? Not necessarily: we remain unwilling to dogmatize about where we are closest to the very words of Jesus and where he speaks in the language of the Church's fervent faith. Instead of deriving our account of Jesus' teaching directly from the gospels, we arrived at it by asking: what is the teaching of Jesus likely to

6. For a fine discussion of these issues, see, besides Niederwimmer, J. C. Fenton, *What was Jesus' Message?* (London, 1971). Both are less cautious than we have been in using gospel sayings as firm evidence for what Jesus taught and, we should maintain, less cautious than they need be to make their central argument hold.

have been to lead to the attitudes which we know from the New Testament to have prevailed in the early Church? This demands no acceptance of particular sayings as authentic: it means rather that certain sayings represent the direction which Jesus is likely to have taken, if the life of the early Church is to be most naturally accounted for. But there is no denying that alternative explanations are available in nearly every case.

If Jesus' teaching was such as we have suggested, and if it was remembered as subordinate to the proclamation of the Kingdom and indeed part and parcel of it, the Church naturally found itself having to work out solutions to many moral problems without guidance from the tradition, and not surprisingly reaching quite diverse solutions. The Church had to build up the rule-book which Jesus had failed to provide, and thereby it imperilled its hold on the clarity of Jesus' message – which was radically distrustful of all such documents. This is, of course, closely linked with the question of whether Jesus foresaw a future of long duration for any community deriving from his work. But on any showing, the Church speedily faced situations which the communities in Palestine had not known, and in changed circumstances came to new conclusions, using other aids (such as the commonplace morals of the day) besides the tradition of Jesus' teaching and being influenced by theological forces which had not operated in the earliest days. The question remains: in these circumstances, in what ways and to what extent did the voice of Jesus remain loud and clear? Or was it soon a cry heard uncertainly and from afar?

5. The Use

How are present-day Christians to use the ethical teaching
of the New Testament? Or in what sense, if any, may that
teaching still be either binding or of more than historical
interest? Whether consciously or unconsciously, many
Christians take it to be wholly binding, for this is entailed by
its presence in authoritative Scripture. Our question then is
part of the wider question: what is the nature of the Bible's
authority for present-day Christian faith? And the answer to
that question will depend upon the acceptance or refusal of
doctrinal assertions about the Bible, and about the whole
idea of canonicity. But however great an authority canonical
status is held to confer upon these writings, it is hard to
carry it into practice in a thoroughgoing way. Even if the
diversity of New Testament teaching is pulped into a
plausible uniformity (e.g. on divorce), and the context
in which the teaching was formulated is ignored, circumstances often make its straightforward following well-
nigh impossible (e.g. on the unquestioning acceptance of
political authority or on the subordinate position of
women) or pose new questions on which the New Testament
offers no direct guidance (e.g. birth control or extermina-
tion bombing). If the modified principle is then put forward – Follow the New Testament as far as circumstances
permit – then another task quickly arises: to formulate a logic by which New Testament teaching may be
applied in unforeseen circumstances. This may work either
by way of analogy (comparison with sufficiently similar
cases on which the New Testament does speak) or by reference to fundamental doctrinal tenets – a procedure adopted

already in the New Testament itself (e.g. Philippians ii, 1–11, urging humility on the basis of Christ's saving work, or II Corinthians viii, 9, urging generosity in the same way). Thus a novel problem may be approached by asking the question: on the basis of what we know of God through Christ what should we now do?

Once this approach is recognized as possible, even necessary, in dealing with *some* problems, it may appear that it should operate in the tackling of *all* present-day ethical questions in a christian context, even those on which the New Testament offers clear teaching which remains wholly capable of being applied. This will be so if the mere word of Scripture is not regarded as binding and if there is a recognition that the New Testament writings have their primary reference to a social and intellectual setting vastly different from our own. Thus, we are commanded to love our neighbours as ourselves, and to bless those who persecute us. These commands are, despite the differences in the circumstances of our lives from those of first-century Christians (e.g. the meaning to be given to *persecution*), as challenging and 'contemporary' now as when they first appeared. They are not addressed to problems raging in the ancient world and long since obsolete. We know what kind of conduct they require of us and our chief difficulty is in doing what we ought. We know that any arguments we might raise about modern life making them peculiarly hard are evasions which could find parallels in any age.

But even in cases like these, ought we not to do justice to the historical and cultural gap between the first century and our own day by recognizing the validity of the following process of thought, even though we are entirely justified in short-circuiting it in practice? Jesus taught thus and evangelists wrote thus in the first century. He taught and they wrote not timelessly, for no man can ever so teach or write, nor even consciously for posterity, for all the evidence is that they believed the End was close, but for audiences of first-century men in first-century settings. His teaching and their writing (and it is the latter alone which *directly* confronts us) rested upon a certain style of relationship with God and, in the case of the books, upon God seen as represented by Jesus and able to be approached through him (a fact capable of a wide range of verbal formulation). To be Christian is at root to share that style of relationship with God which Jesus initiated. What then are its implications for moral life, for our relationships with our fellows, friends and opponents?

In the case of the commands which we took as examples the result of this complex process of re-application will be little different from the simple process of direct reception. But will it necessarily be so in, for example, the case of political obedience or divorce? Let us, following the myth of uniformity, ignore for the moment the diversity in the New Testament's teachings on divorce, and let us suppose that the New Testament simply forbids it. Let us also accept that this ruling was, in the circumstances of the first-century Church, a most appropriate expression of its whole theology and life in relation to marital relations. Does it follow that it remains so in a society where the position of women is different, where the Church occupies a quite different position, where there is a wide penumbra of persons who are partly christian partly not, where social pressures are of a quite different character, and where knowledge of human psychology is much greater? A consideration of all these factors might lead to a conclusion no different from that of the first-century Church, but at least it ought to be reached after a thorough weighing of each of them rather than on the basis of the range of arguments deployed in this matter in the first century (cf. pp. 73ff.). Our consideration of these factors might lead us to adopt a policy quite contrary to that reached by first-century Christians, on the basis of the same fundamental faith as theirs but applying it in a fresh setting. We might even follow the motive of one of them (Luke's compassion, p. 79) to arrive at a policy other than that to which it quite properly led him. (And of course if we now cease to ignore the diversity of the first-century Church we shall not be at all surprised by our conclusion.)

It might be held that another and more radical consideration arises at this point. How far did the New Testament writers fail to pursue the logic of their own doctrine? Matthew, for instance, teaches love not only of neighbours but also of enemies. Yet he hardly maintains this attitude when he confronts the scribes and Pharisees in ch. xxiii; nor, in his picture of final judgement does he show God acting in accordance with this principle; rather, there will be exclusion and punishment for those who merit his rejection (e.g. xiii, 49f.; xxii, 11–14; xxv, 46). This incongruity remains even if it is recognized that he sees the End as a crisis whose uniqueness makes it transcend the morality of every day. Is our response to this to try and make a formula of synthesis which will save Matthew's consistency, or is it the case that because of other features of his world-picture, which he quite takes for granted, he is unable to face the logic of the teaching which in daily human relations he applauds?

Similarly, Bultmann sees the same lack of rigour in Paul, who both demonstrates the total inadequacy of the Law as an ethical principle, substituting for it, on the basis of faith, a demand for radical obedience in each new situation, and yet persists in putting forward rules and lists of moral norms. Bultmann demonstrates the conflict by reference to Jesus' teaching: 'Whoever refuses to dissolve an unendurable marriage by appealing to a word of Jesus; whoever offers the other cheek to one who strikes him because Jesus said so,

would not understand Jesus'.[1] Bultmann's point is not that
such marriages should be dissolved but that refusal to dissolve should not be based on the ground of Jesus' word
which, if taken thus, has lost its character of demand for
radical obedience and turned into law. Now it may indeed
be the case that Jesus' prime concern was not to provide an
amended set of moral norms but rather to face men with
God's sovereignty; but it is hard to believe that the demand
for obedience to a God, whose character is to be recognized
in Jesus, need be as lacking in specific content as Bultmann
seems often to say or that Paul ought to have refrained from
stating it. What is however undeniable is that the return
to the fundamental character of God as the basis of christian
morality means an increasing readiness to seek decisions appropriate in that light and a refusal to accept precedents as
binding.

We have said that the question of the usefulness and
authority of the New Testament in christian ethics is simply
one aspect of its general usefulness and authority. We have
seen that the impossibility in certain cases of applying its
teaching directly, because of changed circumstances, is one
way of showing the limits of that usefulness. The impossibility of deriving precise doctrinal formulation from
the New Testament is another way: clearly, a process of
rationalizing and logical development is (and has been) required to arrive at such formulations in almost every area.
Even the most biblically minded Christian makes artificial
patterns with the texts. What then does the New Testament
effectively provide, in ethics as in doctrine? It yields certain
perspectives, patterns and priorities, and it forms the chris-

1. *Jesus and the Word* (London, 1958), p. 71. However it is equally
true that 'the man who divorces his wife has not understood that
marriage requires of him a complete decision, but thinks of it as a
relative action which can be annulled' (ibid. p. 70).

tian mind which then turns to the examination of contemporary issues – perhaps to apply central New Testament principles more rigorously than any of the New Testament writers. Thus, in matters such as marriage, suicide, homosexuality, war, social intolerance, and the nature of imaginative care for human needs of all kinds, present-day christian moral opinion often displays a subtlety and compassion not found in any New Testament treatment of them, even when they come into view at all. Centuries of christian and non-christian experience, including the emergence of techniques in the human sciences, enable us to deal more christianly and effectively with questions which early Christians either did not face, had no need to face, or else faced only in crude and from our point of view hopelessly oversimplified terms. It is arguable that to be true to the deepest convictions of the leading New Testament writers, and more, to be faithful to the Lord who lay behind them, we need to be emancipated from the letter of their teaching.

At this point we need to face a problem often concealed even in the critical study of the New Testament, that of the role of the canon, that is, the concept of an authoritative body of writings. Whether we accept or reject it, a whole battery of traditional ecclesiastical and literary weapons makes us operate with the New Testament as a fixed and closed body of Scripture, somehow (by the *fiat* of God or the practice of man) to be considered both in isolation from all other writing and as a mass of sheer, unrooted words. It is hard to exorcize all traces of this outlook even when we have in principle come to read the New Testament as something quite different, that is as the bulk of the surviving written expression of the life and faith of the early Church as it witnessed to Jesus. Once we see it from this point of view, we immediately have to reckon with the fact that it is not the whole of the christian literature of the period; its later books need to be put alongside the Apostolic Fathers and even the earlier Apologists, not to speak of writings which bestride the uncertain frontier between Christianity and Judaism (as it was one of the great merits of Bultmann's *Theology of the New Testament* to show). Once we have come to read the New Testament in this way, then its authority as canon has to be seen as, in origin, a particular – and from many aspects a deadening and arbitrary – way of treating this selection of early christian writings, a way which commended itself, for compelling historical reasons (such as the need for fixed authorities to appeal to as standards of orthodoxy in the face of heresy) to the churches of the later second century. No such motives inspired either those who wrote or those who first received and then preserved these books: for them they were, initially, simply writings valued on the basis of their contents, then perhaps of special worth as being, at least by repute, the work of venerated apostolic hands. Not for some generations did they, as a collection, win the status of 'Scripture', alongside the Old Testament, which from the first the Church had taken over in this role from Judaism.[2] It is a pity to be tied to the rigidity of this last view alone.

If we try to see these books as they first appeared – the work of active christian minds answering contemporary needs – we shall be well placed to use them as we have suggested. We shall take each of them independently and resist the canonizing and harmonizing impulse which longs to produce '*the* New Testament view'. We shall let their various colours, some vivid, some duller, but all distinctive, come before our eyes and remain in our minds, affecting and forming them. So the more profound patterns and decisions

2. On this whole cluster of questions, see C. F. Evans, *Is 'Holy Scripture' Christian?* (London, 1971).

of the New Testament writers will, not necessarily determine, but contribute to the work of forming our own
judgements and policies. This will of course depend on the
subject – I Corinthians xiii will determine *tout court*. But
behind the writers is a God who shows up the element of the
provisional in both our decisions and theirs.

The New Testament writings are not simply ancient
books which we now read, as if they had recently been
discovered, long lost, in a library. They have been at their
work of forming the christian mind, along a multiplicity of
logical lines, throughout the Church's history. But beneath
the varied logic, their manner of operating is more allusive,
more all-embracing and more subtle. In her essay, *The Sovereignty of Good* (London, 1970), Iris Murdoch suggests how
'good art shows us how difficult it is to be objective by
showing us how differently the world looks to an objective
vision. We are presented with a truthful image of the human
condition in a form which can be steadily contemplated . . .
Art transcends selfish and obsessive limitations of per-
sonality and can enlarge the sensibility of its consumer. It is
a kind of goodness by proxy' (pp. 86f.). For the Christian,
living, thinking, contemplating and acting within the christian tradition, all this (and more) could be said of the New
Testament (and indeed of other works besides, but the New
Testament is at the head of the stream). The New Testament,
like great art, may act upon a man to lead him to goodness,
not by direct command but by a subtle and complex interaction which involves the New Testament writers' integrity,
and behind them the impulse of Jesus, and the reader's readiness to create afresh out of the material of his own experience. Sometimes this may lead him, on particular issues (like
the ending of an intolerable marriage or the assassinating of
a monstrous tyrant), to a conclusion directly contrary to
that reached by any New Testament writer, but it may

nevertheless have a total christian integrity which obedience to the letter would have betrayed. The integrity rests on constant return to the deepest roots. Behind the ethics of the New Testament lie fundamental moral attitudes, such as that which appears in the gospels as losing life in order to find it. To quote Iris Murdoch again: 'The humble man, because he sees himself as nothing, can see other things as they are. He sees the pointlessness of virtue and its unique value and the endless extent of its demand' (p. 103f.). The Christian could not readily accept this as the whole story, for he sees man as made for relationship with God; yet it is a shaft of light that wants to be seized in its brilliance and not blurred by qualifications. For nothingness is the door to God, and the moral life, as the New Testament depicts it, is marked throughout by that exposure to God which leads a man to self-denial. In so far as it aids that exposure, the New Testament has made its chief contribution to a man's moral growth.

It is at this point that the theological forces, of which we gave an account in chapter 1, can be viewed in their correct light. Time and again, we have seen that christian ethics necessarily involve a 'more than ethical' stance. They are part of the wider business of man's involvement with God. The 'otherness' of God then inevitably 'rubs off' on christian ethics, giving to them, whether in the New Testament or since, always an element of the provisional. This is the religious meaning of Matthew's impossible demand for perfection, as of Paul's sense of the End's approach; of Luke's idealizing of Jesus, as of John's flight from the world. Is it not precisely this element which the forces that we examined (eschatology, the depreciation of the world, the divine authority) were the means of expressing in the religious culture of the first century? Though the forms continually change, that for which they stood is essential to an ethic which is christian – which sets out to bring man to his true bearings in God's world.

Yet equally, in what came to be seen as orthodoxy, those forces could never be allowed to have their head. In the New Testament, here and there, we found signs that one or another of them threatened to drive onwards to its logical conclusion (cf. p. 9). To permit that would be to mistake these particular expressions of God's 'otherness' and of the consequent provisional character of christian ethics, for the transcendence itself. The concern with behaviour in the world is a genuinely christian concern, for the world is God's creation, and the forces which in the first century threatened to minimize and even abolish that concern could not be permitted to triumph in a faith resting on that foundation. Peter Brown points out that in the third century one of the advantages that Christianity offered by comparison with other fashionable cults was 'a way of living in this world'. 'While the oriental cults provided special means to salvation in the next world, they took the position of their devotees in this world for granted.'[3] Already in the New Testament, even in those writers who are most convinced of the imminence of the End, that concern is prominent. Despite the pressures of apocalyptic speculation and incipient gnosticism, even Paul, not to speak of Matthew and the writer of the Pastoral Epistles, are full of serious interest in the problems of daily living in a world where God is sovereign creator. Even in the Johannine writings, where the world-rejecting tendency is perhaps at its strongest, there are theological convictions, which, especially if uttered in an 'off-Johannine' tone of voice, lead firmly in the opposite direction: 'God is love'; 'all things were made through' the Word; 'the Word became flesh'. It was not just the growing

3. Peter Brown, *The World of Late Antiquity* (London, 1971), p. 65.

institutional demands of the Church and the failure of the
End to appear that led to the development of moral teaching.
Jesus' preaching, the character of his work, and practical
needs had produced it, as we have seen, from the earliest
period which we can observe. The conviction that 'God had
visited his people' had injected that concern firmly into the
stream of christian experience.

Yet the God who had visited his people remained beyond
them and 'over against' them, so that always in their policies
and judgements the provisional aspect is inescapable. Regarding the New Testament as canonized scripture may not
unfairly be seen as at least partly one of the Church's many
attempts to evade that element inherent in christian faith
and life; and, closely related to it, so may the treatment of
christian ethics, on a New Testament basis, as a static code.
For all the New Testament writers, ethics do not stand in
their own right but are an expression of the gracious relationship with himself which God has given through Christ.
Paul and John saw this more clearly than any of the rest,
but none of them wholly failed to perceive it (cf. Evans,
op cit., pp. 42f.). We may end where we began: the New
Testament leads one to question the usefulness of ethics as
an object of independent interest. Morality will only be for
man's health when placed in the wider context of his standing in relation to God.

Indexes

NAMES

SUBJECTS

Ethics and the New Testament